BOSWELL

THE STORY OF A FRONTIER LAWMAN

By Mary Lou Pence

CONTENTS

FOREWORD

Nathaniel Kimball Boswell, the newspaper said, was almost eighty-five when he died. He had lived over sixty years in a country to whose colorful history he had added his own footnote. He was in truth an enforcer of law and many frontiers benefited from his unequaled courage and his bulldog tenacity.

Yes, Marshal Boswell was as fearless a lawman as the West ever saw. His life story includes all the trappings of the modern cinema portrayals of the Old West—his Colt and his Henry rifle, his spurs and his faithful mounts. The days of the massacres of the wagon trails by the redmen on the rampage, the Indian wars, the outlaw trails, the gun-scourged rail towns, the range fights. Boz lived through them all. And he played a tumultuous role in them, too! No fiction could possibly excel in dramatic values the romance that presents itself, sheared of all overlay, in the life story of this Old West lawman.

Boz attained the stature of a pioneer who faced a great task in a lawless land. As frontier marshal, he drove out and captured more murderers, horse thieves, train robbers and bad men than any other officer of the Rocky Mountain Detective Association. Unafraid, deadly with a gun, hard as nails, he effectively challenged the outlaw combines which threatened the advance of Western settlement. He meant business when he went after a law breaker. His name brought terror to the most hardened criminals. Subsequently, as Albany County, Wyoming Territory's first peace officer he saw action as the deadshot sheriff of the old Territorial days. Later as Chief of Detectives he served the Wyoming Stock Growers Association in halting rustling, fence cutting and enforcing proper brand inspection.

"There were scars made by arrows in his tough old hide dating from his Indian fighting days, and bullet creases from gun battles as sheriff," said his old comrade Colonel John Meldrum. "He was the only man I ever knew who seemed to be born without physical fear and this is attested to by his hair-raising chances he took in rounding up those notorious desperadoes."

His record was studded with gunfights, but Boz was chary about mentioning killings, even when killing was a regrettable matter of public duty. It was something a modest lawman did not talk about.

You may wonder why his biography remained so long untold. There did appear in the newspapers from time to time incomplete bits of his adventures. And Wyoming history books give him occasional mention. It is from these library and museum files and early days historians' accounts we glean tantalizing fragments—scraps of plots, hints of his courage and endurance and heroism in the conquering of the last frontier in his determination to make a wild land habitable.

W. E. Chaplin, early day Laramie newspaper, wrote: "Without doubt during the time he (Boswell) was sheriff here, and United States deputy marshal and marshal he was the most feared man who desperadoes had to contend with." And Historian Bartlett recorded: "Not to know Mr. Boswell in this state is to argue oneself unknown." That was certainly true in the 1870s and for the next fifty years. But alas, today the fact is that Boz is well-nigh forgotten. As is so often the case a new generation is apt to overlook the real contributors of an era and frequently among them were the peace officers of the wild border country where civil authority had not yet been established and the gun had to be the law.

So for over half a century his story and adventures have been scattered in yellowing newsprint of old papers and in slight sketches of history books relegated to shelves in the archives. Through research and through my contact with descendants and relatives of Boz I collected data. My widespread acquaintance with old timers in my own state, too, paid off. Many, many of them told me, "Boswell? Sure, I remember him. He was one of the bravest men I ever knew. He went hell bent after his man. And he got him, too!"

Boz was a modest man, as are so many men of heroic stature not given to speech, and hesitant about beating their own drums. There was the time he was returned to office as sheriff. A big bonfire lit up Laramie City's busiest intersection and the Fort Sanders Fifth Calvalry band played. Then all the winning candidates took the platform. Judge Melville Brown and Banker Edward Ivinson orated eloquently. But when it came Boz's turn he said simply, "I'm not a man of words. I'm more a man of action, I guess. You elected me to do a job. I'll do my best." And he did. He brought in the Deadwood stage robbers that year. Yes, his record of heroic deeds and bravery speaks for itself.

Boz attained the stature of one of the greatest of frontier marshals by his endurance, determination and simple courage. These attributes should now cause us to look back upon him as a hero. Teddy Roosevelt, who was his friend, was once moved to say, "I like men with guts. I like Boz."

One of twelve children born to respected New England parents, Boz went to work first in the pineries of Wisconsin. He carried with him a minor's release so he could legally collect wages. It was Fate a little later, that forced him to the untamed frontier where life and death for him hung balanced by a hair.

Those were the days when, as Edwin Sabin wrote, "the frontier was like a wild and uncurried mountain wolf, howling all night, every night, and all day as well." Then came the days when the first railroad pushed into the country that was the last stronghold of the plains Indian tribes. The new railheads became spawning places for hard-faced, cut-throat desperadoes. Laramie City was one of the worst, and when the citizens decided the town would have law and order they championed Boz.

"The position is not for a subtle politician. We must have a man unafraid. A man who cannot be bought," the citizens' committee said. And so it persuaded Boz to accept the challenge.

When Wyoming Territory was carved from the wilderness lands and Albany County was designated he became its first sheriff. His domain ran two hundred and seventy-five miles long and sixty miles wide, and it was pock marked with Indian camps and outlaw hideouts.

But before this he'd gained his reputation as an Indian

fighter, a scout, a deputy United States marshal, a frontier detective. In the years to follow his name was to continue to bring fear and terror to the lawless. As sheriff, marshal and peace officer Boz spent his life in the saddle. And when cattle rustling on the Wyoming ranges broke out he was called into the harness by the Stock Growers Association as chief detective. Some eighty deputies were assigned to his vast network.

I write his long overdue story because his name should be among those great lawmen whose courage and fast guns battled so effectively the outlaw bands which flourished during those historic years on the frontier. At times when I was pressed by editors to write a piece on the old West's lawmen it was hard to refrain from putting Boz's story into print in the shorter form. It deserved better.

The one difficult obstacle with which I have been confronted, in the writing of this book, is to provide some of the names of people with whom he associated. At times Boz left only first names or nicknames. Sometimes he hesitated to pinpoint people for fear of embarrassing respectable men whose "black sheep relatives got hanged." Then, too, there has been the dearth of newspaper details. So often these early peace officers were sworn to secrecy. And they themselves often preferred to work without benefit of headlines. They were reluctant to give out names and accounts concerning their captives for fear some member of the outlaw bands would get wind of the whereabouts of their brothers-in-kind and abet a jail break. The Laramie Sentinel of 1878 complained: "We are sorry we cannot provide you more details on the capture of Dutch Charley and his gang." It was not until much later when the lawmen thought the time was ripe that the story was told to the public.

I give this book to you as scrupulously authentic as I could make it. It grew out of long hours of listening to the versions of Boz's acquaintances, and reading all available accounts of his escapades. But most impressive were those reminiscences left by Boz himself when he had grown to be an old man still living in the community he'd made safe. Perhaps it was at a Pioneer Day Celebration, or a reporter interviewing him while he sat on his porch and talked of his harrowing experiences, those crucial moments in which he had been a willing or unwilling participant. I have endeavored to construct the authenticity of his adventures by probing into his letters, his correspondence and from the re-countings of his family's recollections and from memoirs of old timers who knew his way of life.

"He was a man's man," the late Lois Butler Payson wrote me from Bozeman, Montana, " and undoubtedly could turn the air blue . . . Although I was quite young my favorite mental pic-ture of him is of a tall hawk-faced man, his white hair cut rather long, his beard a medium one, standing on the First National Bank corner, and his long beaver overcoat scarcely blows in the wind. He wears a light Stetson, and his dark trousers are tucked into tooled leather cowboy boots . . . My grandfather served in the 1870's as deputy under Sheriff Boswell."

And Harold Hunt of Kansas City told me, "Uncle Kim (as he called N. K.) acquired a large ranch on the upper Laramie River and it was there I spent all my summers as a boy and learned to be a cowboy. N. K. was one of the marshals assigned to escort the newly inaugurated President of the United States, Colonel Theodore Roosevelt, from Laramie to Cheyenne on his 1903 Memorial Day visit to Wyoming. The mounts carefully selected were changed three times during that fifty-mile horseback trek."

Ned Fitch of Laramie recalled some of the hair-raising chances Boz took in rounding up unsavory characters. Mr. Fitch was then a small boy but he and his young friends were often around the courthouse where there was so much excitement. He remembered when Martha Boswell died. "Her funeral for that day and age was the largest one ever held in Laramie."

"And Aunt Mary (Catherine) Erhardt, too," Mr. Fitch re-called. "Boz and Aunt Mary were always chiding each other in their late years about which one would outlive the other. Both had come to Laramie City the first year of its birth. And coin-cidentally death claimed them almost in the same hour of that year of 1921. Two great pioneers, each contributing a role to the winning of the West," concluded Mr. Fitch.

Oda Mason, pioneer rancher, also, told me several incidents concerning Boz. Henry Pope, grand-nephew of Boz, recounted among other things, the hero worship of his generation for the fine old sun-glazed, weather-whipped lawman. Once Boz cau-tioned young Henry about parting his hair down the middle of his head. "It might tag you a sissy. And sometimes it's awfully important for a boy not to be tagged a sissy!"

And Mrs. Pope provided me with a clipping dated October 12, 1921, from the *Laramie Daily Boomerang:* "N. K. Boswell, bravest of pioneers is dead. One of the oldest residents of Laramie died at six thirty o'clock of paralysis. Without doubt during the time he was sheriff here, and United States marshall and deputy United States marshal he was the most feared man who desperadoes had to contend with. And during his long life here Laramie has never been able to point out a citizen more respected, more patriotic and more dutiful. Whenever trouble loomed the cry was 'Send for Boswell.' So highly was the deceased respected, so noble in his life's record and so beloved by all was he that hearts of the entire community are filled with grief at the news of his death."

Yes, the beloved name of Nathaniel Kimball Boswell, Laramie lawman, belongs on the old West roster alongside other dedicated frontier lawmen. Unlike such peace-officers as Oklahoma's Billy Tilghman, Dodge City's Wyatt Earp, New Mexico's Pat Garrett, Tombstone's egrarious Doc Holladay, the career of Wyoming's marshal, N. K. Boswell, was riding with the law, never against it.

The story of Boz is one of Magic—and Fate—and Luck—and Love. His life was filled with excitement and adventure and hardships. Many, many times he was close to death. And he experienced many breath-taking escapes. And always he had the love of one woman.

I have also arranged the details and information in a larger sense to make this a biography of a community, the colorful and robust railtown Laramie, spawned by the great Union Pacific. So intertwined are the records of the two—Laramie and its frontier lawman—that one could not be told without the inclusion of the other. Laramie and the West knew no peace officer more dedicated and more courageous than N. K. Boswell. A gallant man and I salute him!

ACKNOWLEDGEMENTS

The writing of a biography such as this, the life story of one of the most courageous and colorful Old West marshals, N. K. Boswell, is an exacting one. Many people in many places assisted me in one way or another in piecing together the record of this peace officer. And so I make grateful acknowledgment to those who, through inspiration and practical help, have aided me in compiling the raw material which went into this work.

To my husband, who was a personal friend of descendants of old Boz and who urged me to interpret the story of this colorful lawman, I express thanks.

To the relatives of the Boswells now departed this life—Mr. and Mrs. Henry Pope, Laramie, who generously turned over for unrestricted use personal records, clippings and photos from the family archives, and recalled details and anecdotes of Uncle Boz and Aunt Martha; to Lois Butler Payson whose paternal grandmother, Annette Salisbury Butler, was a sister of Mrs. N. K. Boswell, and whose paternal grandfather, Richard Butler, was a long-time deputy sheriff serving under Boz; to Harold Hunt, a nephew of Minnie Boswell Oviatt.

For personal reminiscences and practical help and encouragement, I am indebted to Clarence Boswell Oviatt, only living grandchild of the famed old lawman who penned for me some of his boyhood recollections.

I have had the benefit of rich recollections based on personal knowledge of happenings at the time incidents occurred. I owe much to the memories of those now gone who provided me with bits of information which brought N. K.'s early days into sharper focus; Allan Geddes who personally knew of Boswell's strong opposition to the Johnson County War (that Wyoming showdown between the big cattle outfits and the homesteaders); H. N. Roach, Mattie Wallis, Oda Mason, Henry Amon, Ned Fitch, Thomas Tatham, as well as to the late Jack Costin, grandson of that early-day Laramie lady, Susan Collins Costin; and Russell Thorpe, Cheyenne, who for many years was secretary of the Wyoming Stock Growers Association. The burial records at Greenhill Cemetary, Laramie, were made available to me through the late sexton, Lane Good;

For research and hard persistent digging I owe much to the keeper of the Archives, William Robertson Coe Library, Western History Department, Gene Gressley and his assistants; and to Emmett Chisum of the University of Wyoming library;

I am indebted to the DeGolyer Foundation for perusal of records of the Rocky Mountain Detective Association, an organization of police chiefs, sheriffs and marshals which provided an interstate network of law enforcement agencies dedicated to combating the criminal element that was so prevalent in the early Western territories which in that day were almost totally devoid of law enforcement.

And always when I finish a piece of history, I find it would be incomplete without the help of those hard-working Albany County librarians, Laramie; and those of the Public Library, City and County of Denver;

Also, like so many writers of western stories, I feel a sense of indebtedness to Agnes Wright Spring, Fort Collins, retired from the State Historical Society of Colorado, Denver. I can only add my thanks to those of other writers who regard her with affection as a friend as well as an authority. I found her *Seventy Years, a Panoramic History of the Wyoming Stock Growers* and *Cheyenne-Deadwood Stage* most helpful.

The favors extended me from Edwin Schafer, Director, Union Pacific Public Relations Department, Omaha, Nebraska, have been many. To him I make grateful acknowledgment; as I do also to the keepers of the Carbon County Museum, and to Charlotte Romick, retired Clerk of Court, Carbon County, Rawlins, Wyoming, now of Reno, Nevada; the records in the Albany County Clerk and Clerk of Court offices were made available to me by Minnie Pearson, Alice Cornelius and Zed Gibbs, Laramie;

I appreciate the help given me by the State Historical Society of Wisconsin, Madison, for information on federal census reports and documentary data; and to the Registrar of Deeds of Walberg County, Elkhorn, Wisconsin, for factual information;

For reproduction of many of the illustrations, I wish to thank the Ludwig Photo Enterprises, and Herbert Pownall, photographer, University of Wyoming, Laramie.

I am grateful to all the writers, past and present, who chronicled with care and intelligence that wild frontier era and who chose to mention N. K. in some manner, thus adding important information about him and about those with whom he dealt. I have arranged these fragments of information in what seemed the closest verisimilitude to the life of this courageous lawman, whose impact on the settling of the frontier was profound and enduring.

And lastly, but certainly not least, I thank Nancy McGaw Elliott, Laramie, who extended her expert talent in the typing of the final draft.

The personal cooperation of these many friends and acquaintances has been most gratifying. It is because of their generous assistance I am able to give the completed biography— the story of one of the early West's most outstanding and daring lawmen, Old Boz.

Mary Lou Pence
Laramie, Wyoming

Chapter 1

A GREENHORN GOES WEST

Boz reined his mount to a halt on Boulder Ridge. To the South were the gaunt white peaks of the Colorado Rockies. To the West were the blue and purple masses of Wyoming's Medicine Bows. The nose of his horse was pointed westward toward the new Union Pacific railhead, Laramie City, perched on the Laramie River and surrounded by miles of grass-rumpled plains.

There was little about this man to suggest the puny who'd left the town of Elkhorn, Wisconsin, eight years before. Ever since his near-tragic accident in Green Bay back in 1857, ill health had shadowed his very life. Tormented by lung fever, he had come West to the mountain country on doctor's advice. It was early spring of 1859 when he'd set out with his five gold-seeking companions.

"Gold! Gold!" was their clamor. "Pike's Peak or bust!"

But Boz had no heart for adventure. All this frenzy was something remote, detached, something not concerned with him. When your life is hanging by a frayed thread, what does gold matter?

To appreciate this man who was to become one of the greatest frontier lawmen the West ever knew, it is well for us to review some of the vital statistics and background of this courageous marshal.

Nathaniel Kimball Boswell was born in Haverhill, New Hampshire in 1836. His mother, Lucinda Pike, was a distant cousin of that famed old soldier Zebulon Pike, for whom the peak

1

in the Colorado Rockies was named. His father's forebears came to America during the Colonial times, a refined, educated Scottish clan.

He was one of twelve children in a close-knit family. The father worked hard to give his offspring an education. His mother believed in the cultural aspects of life and reared her daughters and sons to grow up as ladies and gentlemen.

It was only because of the financial strain of such a large family that Boz was permitted at the age of sixteen to drop out of the Academy which he was attending and go with an uncle to the Wisconsin forests. It was here in Green Bay his near-drowning occurred when the small boat, in which he was riding to get out timbers on an island, capsized.

Even at that time something of his tenacious and determined spirit was evidenced when, for fifteen death-freezing hours he clung to the bow of the mackinaw until he was rescued. It was this ill-fated episode which brought on his lung fever and eventually sent him to the mountains of the untamed frontier.

Before he left that February day of 1859 he married his sweetheart of two years, Martha Salisbury of Elkhorn. There were some, no doubt, who thought it strange that he had wed the gentle Martha and almost at once set out on the westward journey. But to Boz and his young bride it seemed the natural thing—like the soldier and his sweetheart, their marriage before the bugles called him to the battlefield. Like the Roman Legions in the times of Maximiamus and Marcus Arelius and Julius Caesar. And who was to say that a future in the wilderness in conflict with violence, wild animals and savages and lust-filled men was not unlike a battleground! Some came back and some did not.

Tales of the boundless realm out yonder had already filtered to civilized America. The Pike's Peak El Dorado. The Bonanza. Great things were happening—fortunes were being made and high adventures were to be had. There were Indians and grizzlies and wolves to fight, and the countless challenges of an unspoiled land.

But all of these things could not stir Boz. Weak and in ill health he had no heart for the adventure. The restlessness he saw in the eyes of others had not yet penetrated his blood stream. The sole reason for his setting out on the trail was health—not wealth.

2

The medicos all warned him that to remain in the East meant resigning himself to a lingering death.

Boz was not a strong man and his racking cough and lack of knowledge of this great outdoors tagged him a greenhorn that first year—a puny completely out of place in this wilderness of rugged devil-may-care race of men.

That trek westward through Iowa and on beyond in '59 had been no kid's play. Bog and mud and swollen streams to cross, wagons stuck and mules balking. Taking his turn as camp cook—ham and flapjacks and stew in the black pot. Striking the tents and harnessing the lead team. Some nights he'd been so weary and sick he could die, but he never let his comrades know it. He kept going. Yes, there'd been plenty of hardships and dangers along the way.

Across the monotonous prairie lands he would gather the dry buffalo dung for fuel to cook the evening meal of beans and bacon and corn pone. And once the Pawnees struck, trying to stampede the horses. Rifles barking and the Indians fleeing full

Indians resent the intrusion of the white man. Original by W. H. Jackson.
Grace R. Hebard collection

speed. Oh, to be sure, he'd learned a lot from those long weeks on the trail. But still he was a far cry from the other gold hunters, ill-prepared for the rugged uncouth life in the mountain mining camps where he was headed.

But somehow he made it, and with his trail companions arrived at Pike's Peak the spring of 1859. From the beginning he tasted the violent life as it was lived in the raw, lawless land.

There was that baptism of blood in the rough camp the first week where he'd witnessed a murder. He'd gone to the shack saloon out of sheer lonliness. A man could always find company there, just sitting around watching the others play cards or noticing the characters who bellied up to the crude plank bar.

Indelibly that night was written on his memory. How he'd taken a turn moving through the loiterers, and the stench of unbathed humanity and stale liquor and tobacco reeked his stomach. He looked around, observing how most still wore their hats pulled down over their eyes, others with their open flannel shirt collars showing unwashed underwear. Hair uncut and matted, and beards grizzled their cheeks protruding bulges with tobacco cuds. He saw none of his former comrades among them and turned to walk away. And then he heard the shot.

Two bearded prospectors quarreling over a claim and a mushroom of acrid gunpowder smoking from a revolver. The falling forward of one of them as from his mouth spouted a stream of frothing blood. And the other dark whiskered man moving back toward the exit, his fingers still on the gun trigger. And no one moved and no one spoke. It was the silence of death. But Boz heard the oath, "This'll teach the sonofabitch to jump my claim." The killer went out into the night, slamming the door as he went. A couple of men pushed forward then and carried the dead man off.

That is how it was on the frontier. Man's country, they called it. Boz, baffled and ill at witnessing his first cold-blooded murder, turned and walked out. He went back to his horse and mule at the fringe of the camp and heavily crawled into his bedroll.

So began the course of Nathaniel Kimball Boswell's apprenticeship in the wild west. So began that difficult, but exigent, change from greenhorn to frontiersman and eventual lawman.

4

Chapter 2

THE UNCURRIED FRONTIER

History has recorded how the publicized so-called "bonanza" proved to be a great disappointment to the eager gold seekers. The region had produced little of the mineral.

"Pike's Peak. Hell. We've been duped!"

And that first year thousands of dispirited and hungry men began the exodus back to "the States." Some of Boswell's trail companions were among them.

But Boz remained. His cool reflection convinced him it was purposeless to expect to reap a fortune, still perhaps he could eke out a living with pick and pan. And already the mountain air was as balsam to his tortured lungs.

He stayed on, lingering in some camp long enough to make a grubstake, hauling logs, helping hoist a cabin. Days when his lungs hurt worse he'd light out alone. Riding up Ute Pass making his bed of "Irish feathers" as the pine boughs were called, and looking at the great canopy of Western sky. It was then when he thought of Martha waiting for him in Elkhorn.

"I've got to whip this. Get well so I can go back," he'd tell himself.

He stayed on and after about a month he decided to try Denver City. It was here he met John Wanless who had a compound of teams and freight wagons, and Jim McNasser who was dealing in frontier real estate. It was the common destiny, enduring the hardships and dangers and privations, that became the basis for their life-long friendships.

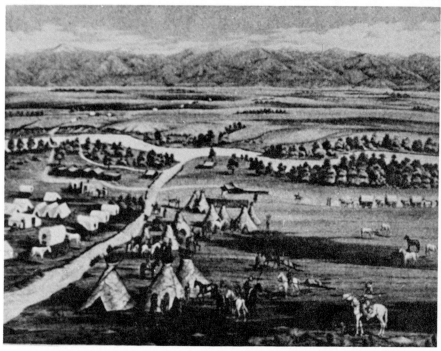

Aurora, Denver City, as Boz knew it in 1859.

And then before the summer turned to autumn, the second excitement came.

"Gold. Gold." A passing miner told Boz about it.

"Twelve miles in the mountains above Denver City. They've really struck it this time. Up in Gregory Gulch on the north fork of Clear Creek."

Boz was skeptical. So were Wanless and McNasser. But the three of them hitched up their wagons and headed for the hills. They came to the Black Hawk camp where the prospectors were pouring in from every direction. For five miles along the narrow, rough trail winding up the ravine were strung shanties, tents and wagon boxes. They found rough hand-sawed boards holding roofs of pine boughs.

There were thousands of men in the Gulch feverishly rushing up and down searching the gravel and the blossom rock. Boz wrote Martha that he'd heard the nuggets were as thick as New Hampshire fieldstones, but he hadn't laid his hands on any yet.

He did file on a couple of claims, then he hired out to McNasser hauling timber for sluice boxes and the quartz mill.

The frosts came early, turning the hillslopes from the lush green to dismal brown. By the last of September, a great raging blizzard descended on the camp. Jim McNasser and John Wanless returned to their families in Denver City. But Boz decided to weather it. He worked all day in the timber and by night he was so tired he could hardly crawl into his wagon box where, with only the sky for a roof, the wind and the cold and swirling snows nearly froze him.

On occasions he'd make it in to Central City and there in Post's General Store along with a conflux of other grizzled miners he'd wedge into the circle around the stove. That's where he met Dave Cook and his younger brother. Three greenhorns they were then, and Dave asked Boz to share their tent back on the Flats. Digging and saving a little gold dust, the men began accumulating a small nestegg.

Gregory Gulch, Colorado, 1859. Boswell spent a winter here.

But Boz disliked lode mining, climbing down the ladder of some shaft where, cut off from fresh air, a fit of coughing was sure to hit him. So he went back to his mules, dragging out timber until he had enough to build a winter shelter house. In spare time the Cooks helped with fitting the logs. Crude, but more comfortable than their Sibley tent.

The Cook brothers kept on with their mining operations while Boz hauled more timber for other prospectors. Thus the amount of gold dust in the secret hiding place was on the increase.

Then one day, a hanger-on got wise to the small cache the men had hidden in the cabin and while everyone was gone, the thief sacked the place. That's when Dave Cook advised Boz, "If you're going to live in this wild land, you'd better learn to use a gun. It's the law of the frontier: 'Protect yourself, kill or be killed.' "

Sunday morning services in a mining camp, Colorado, 1859.

Leslie's Illustrated

So many mornings Boz strapped on his new gun belt, stuffed his pockets with hardtack, packed the mule with a rifle across the saddle and headed for the uninhabited hills. Here he'd practice his marksmanship, punctuating gophers at a hundred yards. And sometimes he'd try his prowess on timber wolves. So, with plenty of shells for his revolver and rifle, Boz reached a turning point in his life.

The winter was a hard one, great drifts of snow piled high around the cabin and the wind tore at the chimney and sent freezing gusts whining through the canvas-paned windows at night. He remained with the Cooks in the gold fields for almost two years. The work was arduous and the comforts few. There was plenty of excitement and danger and hardship. During this interval, he and Dave Cook became close friends and Boz absorbed many of Dave's sleuthing tactics and knowledge of trail breaking. But with the thaws of 1861, the Cooks determined to leave Clear Creek and the mining area and head back to their Kansas farm. They'd had enough, they told Boz, and he was heir to what worldly possessions they left behind. They had an extra team, too, so Boz sold one of his mining claims and bought the horses.

That spring he shifted operations. When John Wanless proposed that Boz go into the freighting business hauling cargo with his outfit operating up and down the Republican River, he accepted—not, however, before he'd been thoroughly warned it was no assignment for a tenderfoot. The Indians were on the warpath and were ambusing and attacking travelers and freighters all up and down the route.

But Boz was no longer a novice with guns. His practice was paying off. He was fast on the draw and sharp of eye and confident he'd be a match for the savages. More than once he got in the thick of it, and there was plenty of it that summer—skirmishes with the Kiowas, the Utes, the Commanches, the Arapahoes and some Cheyennes. The Indians descended with vengence and showed no mercy on the white men who dared invade this land. They killed emigrants and scourged the wagon trains.

And then it was 1862 and the Civil War. But the frontier West was having its share of trouble, too. Outlaws and cutthroats and the Indian menaces. Dave Cook returned from Kansas and took an assignment staffing the frontier forts. Boz joined him.

Attack on a wagon train during the trek west from Iowa to Colorado.

One of his first details was riding out after a Ute who'd stolen their horses. In lonely combat he'd had to kill. The law of the frontier—kill or be killed.

Scouting, freighting, fighting to protect law and property. He was with Cook a year when he met the fire-eating preacher Colonel John Chivington. This Indian-hating man had got them all stirred up. You couldn't witness the Cheyennes on the warpath and the marauding of settlers in Auroria, the isolated ranch families wiped out or living in constant fear of it—and not rise to arms.

"Kill and scalp all Indians, big and little. Nits make lice," the Colonel shouted.

So Boz joined John Evans' One Hundred Days Men and was one in the scouting party sent out to bring in what was left of the Hungates, victims of the massacre on their Running Creek Ranch. They'd been scalped, whacked up beyond recognition, and it was Boz who helped place the remains in the wagon box and drive back the thirty miles to Denver City.

The town officials exhibited the mutilated bodies to the horrified citizens and the Coloradoans rose up in arms. They began organizing a regiment. So Boswell, more scout than soldier, joined the Testament-packing Colonel Chivington and his long splotch of blue cavalry—a sorry assortment of volunteers—marching on the lodges of Black Kettle and White Antelope.

He lived to tell about it later. How it was here at Sand Creek wallowing in his own blood in the icy willow hideout he heard the awful wailing of the squaws and papooses. He heard, too, the death chant of Chief White Antelope and fuzzily supposed it was for him. He did not see the horrors of the sacking of the tepee village. He did not see the old Chieftain shot down. For Boz was one of the first men struck. Poison arrows and whizzing bullets hit him seven times, and he was bleeding so badly he barely made it out of their range. But Sand Creek didn't stop him. The resolve to tame the frontier was now in his blood.

From there he went to scouting the Overland Trail, out of Big Thompson, LaPorte, Virginia Dale and across the aborigine-infested plains to Phil Mandel's on the Little Laramie. Guarding the rocking, rolling Concord coaches in a race for life across the prairie desolation amid sanguinary showers of arrowheads. He could never put out of his mind the sight that day—a wagonload of emigrants had been burnt to a crisp, flames fed by their supply of sizzling bacon.

Violence and greed and lust and hate. And death. It was all here. And for the first time since coming West, Boz wanted desperately to change this savage wilderness, to bring civilization to it.

His health, too, was greatly improved. In the saddle day and night, the high up mountain air and the great open spaces were having the healing effects. So he began thinking in terms of bringing Martha west. If only the Territory would learn some law and order. As it was, the country was practically uninhabited, the governing administration removed and remote, and the dangers were immediate and many. If only they could get some authority in the region then women and children could live here, too.

11

Boswell in his early career on the frontier road shotgun for the Territorial stage lines.

That's when he decided to accept an appointment to Dave Cook's Rocky Mountain Detective corps, a network organized to capture and bring to justice the gangs of cutthroats and ruffians terrorizing the country.

And then it was 1867. A momentous event was at hand. Out of the East could be heard the melodious whistle of the wood-burning locomotive. The black path of the railroad was creeping westward, its steel ribbons dotting the vast acres of wasteland with division points. No longer would this land be known as a crude, uncivilized terrain. There was already Julesburg, now End-o-Tracks town.

No one counted on all the riff-raff that followed on the heels of the rail crews. It turned the budding settlements overnight into Hell-on-Wheels emcampments. Perturbed and angry at the depraved flagrancy of the flotsom and jetsam drifting in, the corps of detectives and lawmen (of which Boz was now a member) kept their hands on their guns. Hell-born Julesburg was a ripper. And

An encampment of Indians on the plains, 1870.   *Smithsonian Institution*

they were calculating that a hundred miles to the northwest, up there on the plains that were as flat as a man's palm, another terminal would sprout. It would be adjacent to the cavalry garrison Fort D. A. Russell and its supply depot, Camp Carlin. This rail town was to be located on Crow Creek where only last autumn the Cheyenne Indians' tepees were staked for the Good Hunt.

The stampede began. The "magic city" Cheyenne enticed a number of early Coloradoans to migrate to its site. Boswell still had his mining claim in Gregory Gulch, but now he traded it for a wagonload of pills and apothecary supplies.

"Hell," Jim McNasser asked him when he heard of the deal, "what do you know about dosing out laudanum and calomel and quinine?"

"Not a damn thing. But I intend to hire someone who does. I've waited a long time to settle down and Cheyenne looks like the place."

So Boswell, in the company of several friends, loaded up following the rutted furrows made by the Holliday sawmill outfit.

He couldn't know then about the trouble that lay ahead. All the lawlessness—with the Dakota legislature in far-off Yanktown buttressing what civil authority it could loan, but not enough. Soon the lootings and terrorizing and killings would convert Cheyenne into a Hell-on-Wheels town, too.

He'd barely got his crude slab drugstore opened for business when Chief Dave Cook of the Rocky Mountain Detective corps came riding into Cheyenne.

"Musgrove and his ring of horse thieves are at large up here. This Musgrove and his lieutenants Sanford Duggan and Al Howard are as slippery as a pack of coyotes, and the syndicate stretches from Texas to Utah. I'm organizing the Minute Men—to be ready on a minute's notice to assist the regular militia of Fort Russell. I'm deputizing you for duty, too."

So Boz leased out his drugstore and joined the Minute Men. It was a full-time assignment, night and day. They caught Musgrove and brought him into the Camp Carlin guardhouse. Some of the men wanted to lynch the bandit then and there, but Judge Kuydendall talked them out of it. A few nights later their prisoner disgorged a couple of window bars and squeezed to freedom. There was a great knot of citizens gathered on Sixteenth Street, chafing and cursing. "Musgrove on the loose again!"

Once more, the lawmen had their work mapped out for them. The alarm came from Jack and Dan Casement's great horse and mule compounds. Musgrove had sneaked down in the dark of night, and raided the freight wagons bound for the Union Pacific grading camps to the West. They made off with the animals, too.

"A hundred head, that's what they got," the contractors reported.

On the heels of this, Captain Mizner at Fort Sanders on the Laramie River sent word that "Musgrove had driven off at least fifty of our cavalry horses last night."

Marshal H. S. Haskell captured Musgrove's henchmen, Sanford Duggan, near Virginia Dale. But a bribed jury turned the outlaw loose, and Duggan fled the country. The laxity of justice chagrined and infuriated the Minute Men.

In the meantime, Boswell discovered Mary Musgrove, the horse-thief's wife, had taken a little house in Cheyenne.

"Musgrove'll be back some dark night," Boswell told Haskell, "so let's keep an eye on her place."

December, 1867, dawned cheerless and dismal, and its gloom was deepened when Martha Boswell's letter arrived telling of her father's sudden death. She'd stay a little longer with her grieving mother—not come to Cheyenne just yet as they'd planned.

New Year, 1868 dawned, and for the marshal it looked as if Cheyenne would never settle down. A couple of hoodlums held up General Dandy and stole his horse and fancy bridle. Another twosome, veneered with their own rotgut, turned on each other. More shooting and one of them killed.

And now Boz had an additional assignment. This time for the railroad: "A band of Sioux raided Elm Station," Union Pacific's Sidney Dillon wired him. " Bring reinforcements before the whole crew is wiped out."

It was here on Cheyenne's Sixteenth Street that Boswell built a drugstore hoping to bring Martha west where they'd settle.

Union Pacific collection

All during the fickle spring months of that year, he was riding long hours, carbines in his saddle boots, revolvers at his sides. In and out of ravines, skirting rounded buttes, scanning scrub pines and aspen groves, sleuthing for Indians. His skin was as weathered and brown as the leather gear beneath him.

Patroling the terrain west of Cheyenne, all along the road-beds from Sherman to Dale City to Tie Siding, he knew the trails as well as he'd known the streets of Haverhill back home. These sullen mountains, these treacherous canyons where wolves and redmen and bandits hid out were now as familiar to him as had been his boyhood fishing holes down at the Great Bend.

Yes, it was over eight years that he'd been on the frontier. Eight years. That was a long time to be committed to risk and danger and hardship. It was a long time to keep a wife waiting. But now there was no turning back. His roots had taken hold.

Chapter 3

A MARKED MAN

Through the high country with its broad expanse of undulating plains in what is now southeastern Wyoming, the Union Pacific in the spring of 1868, its steel ribbons like earth worms, pushed forward. Already an encampment of prospective settlers waited on the banks of the Laramie River. Here a new terminal, Laramie City, was to be platted.

By the time the rails arrived, there were a few scattered road ranches. Boswell's old friend, Phil Mandel, was running the Overland Stage stop on the Little Laramie. And the Widow Catherine Erhardt, whose husband had died on the trail west, had arrived with her small child and two milch cows, and staked out land along the river. Jackson Brown and John Keene had already settled on choice plots. There were many acquaintances—Ed Ivinson, Simon Durlacher, George Fox, John Wanless, Noah Wallis, and S. W. Collins as well as Fort Sanders personnel Michael Carroll, John Connor and Morgan Knadler and other traders and soldiers from the army garrison. The town was to be designated within the boundaries of this frontier post.

When the agent arrived and announced land for sale, there was a wild rush for filings. Boz was among them, selecting a lot on Second Street. His drugstore in Cheyenne had been a good investment, so he decided to repeat the venture in Laramie City. He could lease it to Pharmacist Hewitt until Martha arrived. He was then free to go back repping for the law as border detective and marshal.

Now it was midsummer, 1868, and his Laramie friends had

17

The Cheyenne Minute-Men fight off an Indian Attack as the Union Pacific constructs westward.

A scene depicting the coming of the rails to the Wyoming plains.

sent for him. Major Tom Sears, appointed sheriff of Dakota Territory of which the new county was a sub-division, had his hands full.

"It's the worst burg on the Union Pacific," he told Boz, "all the provisional officers have resigned, and the cutthroats have taken over. The citizens are scared out of their wits—all the killings and hold-ups. Something's got to be done!"

"If we could get some law and order here," Merchant John Wright told him, "we could have a good town. We're organizing a citizens' committee and we need your help. You've done it before—North Platte, Julesburg, Cheyenne, Dale City."

In later years, Boz was to recall the night he made his momentous decision to join the town's Citizen Committee. He was to learn a lot that night: How Mayor Melville Brown and his town officers had resigned after only three weeks; how the outlaw Asa Moore had taken over, naming his equally tough confederates, Long Steve Young, Big Ned Wilson and Con Wager as deputies. Another desperado, he'd empowered as town marshal.

"This fellow," Sheriff Sears told Boz, "was run out of Denver and is teamed up with Asa Moore. I tell you it's something—the bar fights and street brawls and robberies. It's a dead ringer for Julesburg."

And now Boz was on his way to Laramie City. On the precipice of the trail which overlooked the town, he could see lights splashing and blinking through the grey veil of the evening. Just ahead of him was a column of horsemen, like a great snake twisting along the crooked road in silence except for the clop-clop of hooves and the creaking of saddle leather, and a few words spoken in low, gruff tones. They were the cavalry lads from the Fort stirring the dust as they headed into town to whoop it up.

Before him to the West, he could see the facade of crude buildings facing the railroad tracks. As he neared the outskirts, Boz noticed how the lights shimmering golden in patches spilled from the tents and shacks. He could hear all that revelry coming from some thirty saloons, gambling dives and brothels.

The hurdy gurdy grew louder. The monotonous drone of the keno callers was like a bass drum accompanying the shriller

19

Frank Leslie's Illustrated

**Early settlers hewed up cabins on the river bank waiting the arrival of the
Union Pacific rails.**

sounds—the high pitched staccato of those girls and the cursing
of the riff-raff.

All up and down the streets the immigrants wagons and
oxen freight outfits lined the way. There were teamsters and
grading crews and timber workers with payday money bulging
their pockets, milling about ready to sample the town's night life.
And newly arrived settlers with a nestegg to tide them over.
There was a sharp crack of a Winchester on the night air,
answered by a pistol shot. Boz held a tight rein on George for his

mount was acting up, nervous and skittish. He headed for Guinan's livery barn, where he stabled his horse, then walked to the corner of "B" and Second streets.

Laramie City in full boil. He could hear the rowdiness coming from the Belle of the West, fanciest of the ill-famed dives, and the huzza from the Diana and from the Bird of Paradise running it a close second. Yes, Boz'd seen their likeness in other towns, saloons rubbing shoulder to shoulder. Rowdy tenderloins, women plying their trade where men had easy money. Men sallow of complexion, flabby of face, paunchy of belly. And the Big Tent of ill-fame following the rails. But by now, the Big Tent had moved on westward—to Benton City. And Boz had assumed that most of the ruffians would follow it. Looked like he'd guessed wrong. At least the fellows back there at the stable were saying the slogan in Laramie City was still "A man for breakfast every morning!"

The **"Big Tent," a den of iniquity, followed the rails as terminals sprang up through Colorado and Wyoming Territories.**   *Union Pacific collection*

As the minutes wore on, the raucous noise became louder. Then sharp on the night air came the ripping sound of gun blasts. As Boz stood watching, a man likkered to the gills came staggering out of the Belle of the West.

Yes, it was like the citizens said—the hoodlums had sure taken over. There was no doubt about it—they'd put the fear of God into the town's officials, and now the self-appointed thugs were having things their way.

Boz sauntered down to the Railroad Hotel, that two-story extension of the Union Pacific depot which ran along Front past "B" Street. He was just about to turn the knob on the big door when a man sidled up to him.

"New to town?" Boz took a good look at the fellow, his sloping forehead, his beady eyes. "Let me tip you off, stranger," the man persisted, "Boss Asa like you to spend your money in his place. Everyone plays cards at the Belle of the West. See you there a little later."

Boz faced the man and his eyes were cold as steel. "The hell with Boss Asa. I'll pick the company I keep."

Boz turned then and went inside the Railroad Hotel, where his old friend Jim McNasser was putting up.

"I knew you'd come, N. K." McNasser strode over and shook hands. "I told John Donnellan so. He's wanting to bring my Marian here to settle. But it's like I told him—Laramie City is sure no place for a lady. Now how about having supper with me?"

Boz said he really ought to go over and see if his own shanty on Second was still there, but he was hungry and so the two friends sat down to a meal of fried potatoes and antelope steak.

"Saw Steve Young sidling up to you outside," Jim said. "A tough hombre if there ever was one. Only take it slow—that's my advice to you. This high up air does something to a man's blood. Puts temper and impatience in it. A man has to watch himself." Then he changed the subject. "Where you stopping, Boz? The town is chuck full, but you're welcome to bunk here with me."

Boz wished he could have taken Jim up on the invitation, but he really ought to look the town over. So he thanked Jim and headed out into the night.

How long Boz walked up and down the streets, he wasn't

sure. But it was getting late when he ran into Hewitt, who'd leased the drugstore. "You're welcome to spend the night in my place. I've partitioned off an extra room."

The lawman accepted, as it had been a long day and he was dead tired. He lay on the bunk, mulling over in his mind what should be done. How to go about making the town safe? As it was, it sure looked like the devil was taking good care of his own kind. From across the street, the dance hall music kept interrupting his thoughts. The whine of a fiddle, the guffaws of rowdy men, the coaxing prattle of the women. One in particular kept punctuating the din, "To the bar, Paddy, don't be stingy with your money."

Since he couldn't sleep anyhow, Boz got up, struggled into his pants and boots and hitched his gun belt on. He moved stealthily out into the night.

He was barely outside when something came sailing past him. It was an old man, landing head first in the mud-churned street. He saw the man roll, lose his breath in a long, strangling sound. Silhouetted in the doorway was another form, apparently the one who'd done the booting. This fellow went back inside, slamming the door behind him. Boz walked over to the prostrate form, but on first glance, saw it was all over. The old man's skull was bashed, his pockets turned inside-out. The sign on the building from which it had all happened read, *Belle of the West*. Still alone, Boz walked over, turned the knob and went inside.

He was right. The villain was Steve Young, the man who'd cornered him at the Railroad Hotel. The desperado was heading back to the bar, wiping his apron and picking up a bottle and pouring a big drink.

But there was another man, the tall swarthy one, that now attracted the attention of Boz. This fellow was leaning over an unconscious young soldier. There was a gash in the kid's head from which blood spurted. The man was counting a roll of bills. When he finished, he straightened up and Boz saw the badge—a lawman's badge. The fellow had not seen Boz. He was turning away from the kid and swaggering back to the bar and Steve Young. He began dividing the sheaf of bills with Steve.

"Good work, Sam," Steve Young smacked his lips and held out a bottle of whiskey to his confederate. But the man called

Sam had turned and in short, quick strides was hurrying back, stopping only when he reached the short-skirted, paint-faced girl, his magpie eyes flashing fiendish-like. The girl was still bending over the unconscious young trooper. The man called Sam, his eyes still dark and serpentine, jerked the girl upright. "You little bitch," he said, slapping her hard across the mouth with his hand. He hit her hard again. "Mebbe this'll learn you to meddle in my affairs."

Then he reached for his holster, bringing up his gun.

The woman screamed. The same shrill screech which had earlier awakened Boz. The man lifted the gun and swung, its handle making a loud thud as it hit the girl's head.

"And let this be a lesson to you—keep out of my affairs," his voice was gutteral and churlish. The girl slumped to the floor, but the beady-eyed Sam pulled her back up by the hair, throwing her into a nearby chair. As he did so, he faced the door and Boz got a good look at him. In a flash it came to Boz he'd seen the man before. More than once.

He was Sam Duggan, the same desperado who'd killed a man at Granite Canyon. The same whom Haskell had shackled up in the Camp Carlin guardhouse. The henchman of the horse thief, Musgrove. Sam Duggan. Now marshal of Laramie City.

And tonight this same Sam Duggan was beating the daylights out of a woman. Boz moved quickly, his guns in his hands. Not that he had any respect for the woman, still he was not going to stand idly by while Sam Duggan beat her insensible.

His hands on his guns, he walked unafraid toward Duggan. "Let the girl go, Duggan," he said, and his voice was quiet, but it had a cool, deadly sound. His piercing eyes were fixed on the outlaw. For a moment the startled Duggan returned the steady gaze. Then his shifty eyes dropped and his clutching fingers gave up their hold on the girl. Cringing and whimpering, she slumped into the chair. A little later, she slipped out a back exit.

Still holding the bead on Duggan, Boz backed his way toward the street entrance. Behind him, he heard the door open. Then he heard voices and recognized them to be his friends, Major Sears and the auction house dealer "Cheap" John Wright, their guns cocked and aimed.

Boswell said, "The kid over there. The one in the uniform. Help him out of here."

Afterwards, Boz was to marvel that he had lived through that night. Duggan, as town marshal, had a dozen deputies as corrupt and vile and desperate as their boss. But for some reason, they had not been around.

Boz and his friends retired to Wright's auction house to discuss the desperate affairs in Laramie City.

"There's a lot of things happening here that's hard to believe," Tom Sears said. "Men with sizeable rolls go in Asa Moore's place to play cards disappear out the back door to be hauled away to a gully. Robbed. Killed."

"I think it's about time the citizens of this community get organized to protect themselves and their property," Wright suggested.

"It will take a lot of doing," Boz, his lean fingers stroking his chin, said. "We can't expect honest men to bring families here to settle in a place like this." So the men agreed to meet the next day with a dozen others and plan their strategy.

The grey, late summer dawn broke sometime a little after four o'clock and Boz returned to Druggist Hewitt's annex. The town slept now, but for the lawman, there was little rest. While his host slumbered, Boz got up, dressed and went out into the morning. He passed Guinan's corral, Whipple's blacksmith shop, and Henry Wagner's store. Then he went toward the pine-boarded Worth Hotel. He'd breakfast there.

As he walked, the town began awakening. A switch engine whistled and he saw railroad workers coming off their night jobs. Ox-drawn freight wagons were lining Second Street ready to pull out. At another intersection, ties and lumber were piled in great blocks. Here and there, buildings were going up, the pounding of hammers and buzz of saws were a part of the morning confusion. Five thousand people were now residents of the town, they told him.

As he turned a corner, he saw a man come riding hard down the street. The horse hit a mud puddle and headed for Catherine Erhardt's milk cart. With a shove of his boot, the man gave the wagon a push and it went toppling over, the precious milk cover-

25

ing the ground. Just then the lawyer Melville Brown, the town's plagued first mayor, came up and stood alongside Boswell.

"I'm glad you came, N. K. See what I mean—that was Con Wager, the thug. This kinda stuff, and worse, going on all the time. Something's got to be done. Make Laramie City a safe place for women and children."

The two men parted, and Boz entered the hotel. Outside, a bullet ripped the air. A freighter with his six mule team was cursing his string. The wheels of the freight cars on the curves heading northward, howled and the steam from an engine sent its sputtering sound on the high wind.

Yes, Boz had made up his mind. He'd join the Committee and help clean up the town. He would have to write Martha and postpone her coming just yet. The town had to be tamed. Besides, he was already up to his neck in trouble. You just didn't call Sam Duggan's hand and expect to get away with it. Yes, he was a marked man. It was him or Duggan.

Chapter 4

BEGINNING THE CLEANUP

Recalling the night he'd encountered Sam Duggan at the Belle of the West, Boz never was certain how he'd managed to stay alive. Catching Duggan off guard when his henchmen Moore, Wager and Big Ned Wilson were elsewhere, had certainly been a boon. And Long Steve Young, had for some reason, seemed disinclined to blow the daylights out of him that night. Maybe he'd seen Boz's hand tightening on the gun.

Charley Hutton, pulling in early next morning with his freight wagon, supplied the answer to Asa, Con and Big Ned's whereabouts the night before: "They ran off a bunch of my stock. Them and Musgrove. Their horses all caked and played out this morning are over at the Excelsior."

Hutton had the Big Laramie Overland Stage stop seven miles out of Laramie. Since the stage had quit running a few weeks back, he'd been freighting meat and vegetables out of Colorado to Fort Sanders and the railroad camps to the West. He still ran his roadhouse for the convenience of immigrants passing through. And lately he'd been using his corrals for beef on the hoof and for fresh horses for the Pacific-bound travelers.

Hutton came into Laramie to proposition Boz. "Things are getting pretty serious—what with both the Sioux and the horse thieves on the prowl. How about you joining me? You know the country like a book, and the job would sure give you a chance at Musgrove's horse thieves."

And so Boz gave Hewitt a renewed lease on his drugstore and began freighting again. That's how he came to know Captain

Allen Reed, an important surveyor and contractor for the U.P. One of Reed's big tie camps was on the Laramie, and Boz agreed to supply it with fresh meat and vegetables.

One evening Boz, riding into camp with a wagon load of provisions, found the Captain and his timbermen awaiting him. The usual boisterous brawling hacks were quiet and serious tonight. As he joined their circle, they sat whittling—not glancing up. It was Captain Reed speaking, his voice belying his emotions and grief.

"My son, Robert, they killed him. And shot up his friend. Jimmie's real bad in Laramie City. The kids just went into town with their pay checks. They didn't have a chance against those killers. There's no law here, so I went out to Fort Sanders for help. But the Commandant said his Cavalry and Infantry companies were out chasing Redskins. Besides, he has no jurisdiction over Laramie City. And while the Sioux are cutting the telegraph wires, Asa Moore's hirelings are cutting our kids' throats."

Yes, evidence was everywhere that the self-appointed officials—paunchy and pink-cheeked Asa Moore, mayor; ape-faced Long Steve Young, justice of the peace; shifty-eyed Sam Duggan, town constable, and his deputies Big Ned Wilson and Con Wager assisting—ruled supreme.

Boz looked away from the grief-stricken father and began stroking his chin. "We'll see. There must be something, some way to halt this murdering."

That night in Laramie City, Boz walked down Second Street. As he talked to leading citizens, he saw their lips grow tighter. In their eyes was the pinch of uneasiness and despair.

Boz's drugstore was right in the heart of the rowdy tenderloins. He was there with Druggist Hewitt next morning when a man in baggy pants and silk shirt came in. Hewitt introduced him, "Ed Franklin. And what can we do for you today?"

"There was an accident on the street day before yesterday. A boy pretty bad shot up. We rushed him to the first aid house, and I'm elected to take up a collection for his care. If we get Doc Finfrock right away, the boy might live."

Hewitt nodded. "Sure, I'll chip in." Boz reached into his pockets and brought out some bills. Two employees and some customers said they'd donate, too.

"Here—almost eighty dollars," Hewitt said, handing the money to Franklin. Boz turned then and went back to the rooms behind the drugstore. From outside came the sound of saws, the din of hammers, the smell of fresh lumber. It reminded him that the time had come to replace the canvas roof. Something more permanent before the early winter blizzards sent the snows whipping in. He had a couple of free days before he and Charley Hutton would hit out again with their teams.

He began assembling his tools—hammer, saw and nails. Up the ladder he went.

His drugstore was right in the heart of the rowdy tenderloins, where about every other business establishment was a deadfall. By the time the August sun sent its streaked crimson complexion over the town, he'd finished the roof. Then he sat down to write Martha a letter.

As he wrote, there came to him through the open window, the clatter of hooves, the blast of guns, a man's terrified yell, a woman's shrill scream, a chorus of guffaws. Yes, Laramie City, with nightfall had come alive, its ribald populace seeking to satisfy lusty appetites.

He could not bring himself to write Martha about conditions in Laramie City. Nor how the Bosses Five ruled the town. Five men with the very devil in them. She would worry. But he wrote her that they'd have to postpone her coming West for a little while. That the frontier was still no place for a woman.

"It's a big country out here. Bigger than the whole New England and right now it's in a state of coming and going. It'll settle down, though, one of these days. Won't be much longer. Then you can come."

While he was writing, Pat Doran of the Shamrock Hotel came in. "Boz, I just stopped in to tell you I heard Asa Moore talking to Con Wager. He told him that one of Cook's detectives had just hit town. That he'd heard you had orders to put the lid on. They don't like you meddling in the town's affairs. You better go slow and careful. You're a marked man. And beware of the woman, Diane. She's Asa's wife or paramour, and runs one of his places."

"I've never hit for brush yet," Boz said. "But thanks just the same."

The next freighting trip with Hutton took Boz out of town for almost a week. The first morning of his return, Captain Reed, livid with anger, came into the drugstore annex, getting Boz out of bed.

"Come with me, Boz. I want you to have a look at Jimmie, the kid they shot up the day they killed my boy—the one Ed Franklin and Sam Duggan went around collecting money for. Just come with me."

Boswell dressed and the two went out the back door, heading north. At the end of the alley they turned east on "A" Street. On the corner facing Third squatted a little log shanty. Originally it had been the jail, but with Asa Moore having his own private hoosegow back of his barroom, this one had seen little use.

The heavy knob gave under the pressure of Reed's fingers and the men walked inside. It was dark and dank smelling. On a cot against the wall a youth tried to raise himself, but fell back, writhing in pain. Boz saw blood oozing in spurts from the boy's shirt.

"Jimmie," Reed questioned, "has a doctor or anyone been in to see you?" To the question, the boy faintly answered, "No doctor has come. But two men came and they took what little money I had left."

"Which two men?" Boz wanted to know. He had to lean down to catch the lad's gasping reply. "The two who killed Robert and shot me. They called each other Ed and Sam."

Boz straightened, "I'll see about this. Captain, you go fetch Doc Finfrock and I'll wait until you come back. But hurry."

The morning sun was coursing its way in the August skies over the town when Boz left the boy in the medico's care. Up and down Second Street Boz went, asking merchants and citizens, "How much did you subscribe for the lad's care?" Some gave their contributions to Ed Franklin, others to Sam Duggan.

Boz headed for the Belle of the West. He was walking rapidly when a friendly hand slapped his shoulder. Wheeling around, he was face to face with Asa Moore. "Boz, I'm sure glad you're back from Colorado. Tomorrow is election day and I want your help."

Boz sputtered his wrath. "I'll help you all right. I'll help you lose the election, that's what I'll do."

30

"What's that? What's that you're saying," Asa feigned surprise.

But Boz, red with rage, had only hot words for Duggan and Franklin, and what they'd done. "I've inquired about the sum they collected for treatment of the wounded boy. Over 270 people subscribed and not one penny of it has gone for Jimmie's care. Fleeced the merchants, that's what you men did. I intend to call Duggan and Franklin to account."

Asa jutted out his chin defiantly, "You leave Sam and Ed alone. I won't have you making charges against them. Do you hear?"

About this time, Duggan appeared on the scene. Boz accosted him. "What'd you do with that money you collected?"

"It's none of your damned business what I did with it. And you keep your goddamned nose out of my affairs or you'll wish you had."

A crowd was gathering now to see what was going on. Boz saw the faces of honest citizens and many of his friends. Then Doc Finfrock arrived and informed them that the lad Jimmie was dead. Boz pulled a dry goods box out away from the building and climbed atop it.

"You heard the Doc. This man Duggan has taken your money that you raised for the lad and pocketed it. What is your wish in the matter?"

"Hang him! Hang him," someone shouted. Soon the chorus grew in volume. "Let's all hang him. Let's hang him!"

Another voice was rising above the din now. It was that of the lawyer, Melville Brown. "No! Listen to me. Let's not hang him. Let's give him fifteen minutes to get the money back to us. And another fifteen to get out of town."

Asa Moore saw the sea of angry faces. He saw the hatred in the eyes of these men as they turned to Duggan. And he heard the shouts grow to a great clamor. "Fifteen minutes. Just fifteen minutes."

Asa's pink cheeks paled now and his water-weak eyes wavered. But motioning to Duggan, he ordered loudly, "Go and get the money, Sam. Bring it back here and give it to them." In a flash Duggan was gone, disappearing inside the Belle of the

West. In double time he was back, thrusting a wad of bills at Asa, who in turn handed the money to Boz.

"They'll make up for it tonight in their Bucket of Blood," someone predicted. And then one of the townsmen had an idea, "What you say, citizens, that we make sure Duggan leaves Laramie?"

But when the men went inside the saloon, Duggan was gone. "Let's satisfy ourselves we've seen the last of him," one man suggested.

"Sure, let's give him the pleasure of our company," they chorused. Volunteers gathered around Boz. They headed toward Andy Guinan's stable.

"There he goes," someone yelled. "Riding that roan." Almost in the same instant, Sam Duggan saw them and spurred his mount to a gallop, lashing madly, heading out Third. In a flash his pursuers, now mounted, were hot on his trail. He was in shouting distance when Boz called, "Halt I say, or we'll shoot."

Duggan saw the odds were against him and that the men meant business, so he obeyed the order.

"We've decided to escort you," Boz, official spokesman for the Laramieites, told the outlaw. "Make sure your days here are done."

Out past the military reservation, they rode, past the verdant bordered springs, over the sun-dried prairie. Ten miles. Fifteen miles. Then they hit for the wooded area of the Wyoming Black Hills.

"You have one alternative," they told the bandit. "If you keep going and never come back, we'll let you go. But if you're ever caught in our town again, it's a rope around your neck."

There was no doubt that these men meant business and Duggan knew it. They watched him go until the wooded Sherman area closed him from sight.

When the posse returned to the Belle of the West to deal with Franklin, they learned that the outlaw had hit for cover. No one knew where he'd disappeared.

It was a few days later that the Fort Sutler, John Wanless, brought news: "We've got Ed Franklin shackled at the army guardhouse. I've got no respect for Franklin," Wanless said, "but, Boy, you'll have to hand it to him—his scrappiness! Guess you

Fort Sanders, guardian of the Overland Trail and the Union Pacific rail builders. Its corrals were raided regularly by the horsethieves.

heard about him holding those seventeen blue coats at bay all by himself."

The soldier, Mike Carrol, helped fill Boz in on that escapade. "When Franklin left Laramie City late that night, he teamed up as Musgrove's henchman. Stole a band of army mules right from under our nose. We chased him clear out on the prairie. Had him cornered, too, when I'll be damned if he didn't scrape up a barricade of sand, hid behind it and poured lead at us like a hailstorm. We gave it right back to him. But for over an hour, he held us at bay. Then some of our bullets struck home. After that, it was easy."

"He's nearer dead than alive, though," Wanless put in. "He'll cash in his chips in short order."

But Wanless was wrong. A few days later, the fort and the town were startled by the news Mike Carrol brought! When Doc Latham went in to dress Franklin's wounds that morning, he found the cot empty. Franklin had escaped.

By September, the surrounding hills were touched with russets and yellows. Sometimes, wandering down by the river to Doc Shores' camp, Boz would hear the chirp of crickets. How soon they'd die their deaths in the first autumn frosts.

33

Union Pacific collection

The Citizens Committee gather at the hanging of Long Steve Young. The boy, Billie Owen standing beside pole, lived to tell of the historic event many years later.

Chapter 5

A NIGHT TO REMEMBER

It was still early that October morning and Laramie City slept. Suddenly from down the street came the boom of a shotgun blast, and Boz was out of his blankets with a start. His room was cold, for this first dawn came not sunny and warm, but full of gloom and shadows. His eyes went first to his saddle rifle. It was still there over in the corner. And his sixguns hung within an arm's reach at the head of his bed. Lately, he'd come to thank his lucky stars when he awoke in the morning to see a patch of early sunlight break through the square of the window. The sudden awareness that he was a marked man had put a wariness in his conscience.

Boz, up now, pulled on his trousers and boots, washed his face and then sat down at the table. A stack of unopened letters were still piled on it. Boz picked up one. It was from Dave Cook.

"The horse thief, Musgrove, is on the loose again. And Sam Duggan and Ed Franklin are teamed up together. A part of Musgrove's network now. I hear those two are somewhere up there where Sherman Ridge cuts off the Laramie plains. Your work's cut out for you."

Boz hadn't planned on this. At least not until the committee had cleaned up Laramie City. Well, Musgrove would have to wait.

Going down to the Worth Hotel for breakfast, Boz ran into Tom Sears and Doc Shores. "Somebody's run off my bunch of wild hosses," Doc told Boz. "Them I had corraled to take back to Missouri. And Uncle Ben's been shot, left barely alive when I

35

found him. His freight wagons ransacked, too. Fifteen wagons without hosses. Stranded. That's what I am. That's the fix I'm in."

Uncle Ben was Doc Shores' bullwhacker. Had been for years now making the drives from Missouri to the Pacific over the Overland. Boz could see the men gathered around Doc were worried and anxious. Valentine Baker coming in added to the seriousness, "We found some bodies this morning in a box car, garroted and bullet riddled. And Harper here was in the Belle of the West last night when Asa Moore hit a man over the head and Con Wager came up behind the guy and rolled him. They picked his pockets and Long Steve finished him and hauled him off to their morgue."

"The time has come, Boz," said Cheap John Wright. "We've got a dozen hand-picked men. The town's leading citizens—men who are fed up, have had enough of the leeches like Asa Moore and his hirelings living off honest people. We've set the time and place. Be there tonight."

And so the citizens' committee went to work. Men who had come to grow roots in Laramie City; men with families, men like Boz. Men driven to the last resort in their efforts to make Laramie City a respectable place.

"Boz," Cheap John said, "You organize the squads. You have know-how. The rest of us will take care of other details."

Silently, systematically, the plans were made. The night was set. It was to be timed like clockwork. The raid on the hellholes. Some five hundred of the town's best men assigned to squads with orders to descend simultaneously on twenty of the town's worst hangouts. The date—October 18. Target number one was to be the Belle of the West, and ranking alongside it was the Bird of Paradise.

Twilight came and went. It left in its place the beginning of nightfall, the air was quiet but grimly expectant. All along "B" Street, the window shades were drawn, the doors closed. The streets were empty. Down by the depot, the train's engine spotted its fitful headlights over the town. The dark of the night was deepening, and with it came the usual hurdy gurdy and rowdy talk from the vice-holes. A fiddle whined and a piano thumped. "March up to the bar, Paddy. Don't be stingy. A drink. A drink."

And then it happened. A rifle shot ripped the air. And then

another. Trigger-fast on the night wind came a barrage of pistol shots and the staccato of fast running feet.

And now, Boz with his squad of men hunched up and crouching whispered, "Something's gone wrong. They weren't suppose to give the signal for another hour. The squads aren't ready to hit all the spots yet. Well, it's done. It's them or us now. Work fast."

John Wright came rushing past Boz. "Damn it. Tom Sear's gun went off accidently. Then Wager shot back. Now the ruffians are up to us." The racket of gunfire dimmed his voice.

Boz shouted, "Get those five." The squad began racing. Wright had a coil of hemp and Al Huston was helping him along with it. The citizens were converging from all directions—on the run. The racket of gunfire was almost deafening as they moved into the Belle of the West. Bullet for bullet, trading lead for lead.

Outside the darkness of the night deepened and an unwonted quiet came over the town. Inside the Belle of the West a lamp on a table cast a sallow glow over the room. White-faced women in gaudy dresses who, an hour ago, had sat on high stools and dealt blackjack now were scrambling out the back door, out the windows. A man lay chest down on the floor, his face twisted to one side, and around him was the dull shine of blood.

The breath of a bullet licked Boz' face, but the slug struck in the wall behind him. Boz dropped to the floor—his lean body flat against the planks and with a quick shot from his revolver, shattered the lamp. Around him were repeated gunshots, outlaws taking one last blast at a citizen he'd spotted. The smell of powder smoke was thick. Then it was quiet.

Boz groped his way toward the door. Someone bumped into him, and with a low curse, the man rushed on. Then Boz saw the coil of hemp and citizens working fast, tying up this man—Con Wager. Another squad had its prisoners in tow—Asa Moore and Big Ned Wilson.

Someone said, "John Keene's barn. It's not finished, but the cross rafters are up."

The squad began moving, pushing their captives ahead. Every time one of them seemed inclined to balk, a committeeman jabbed him in the ribs with a rifle. They moved fast, down the al-

Western History Research Center, University of Wyoming
The hanging of the desperadoes: "Big Ned" Wilson (alone). Asa Moore and Con Wager (back to back—Wager in shirt sleeves).

ley behind Second, heading for South "E." They came to the un-finished log barn.

There was a cross lintel. A couple of men tossed the rope end over it. "Nine feet. Just right."

"Get 'em up by the necks," someone ordered.

"But we've got only three of the thugs. Where's the other two?"

"One of them is dead, back there on the floor of the Belle of the West, plumb full of bullet holes. The other, Long Steve Young, got away."

The men pushed their prisoners inside the logged up walls and began going about their grim business. First, they hoisted up

Big Ned Wilson. He swung alone from one rafter. On another beam, they threw the noose for Con Wager, still in his shirt sleeves.

"Move him over," one man said. "Make room for his pal." The noose was tightened around Moore's neck. The veins on his bald head began showing. "We'll hang these two together—partners in crime, so let 'em be in Hell."

That was when Asa began begging. "I promise to leave town and never molest you again."

"You had your chance," the committeemen chorused. "You should have left with Sam Duggan."

"Please, then, men grant my last request. Take my shoes off. My mother always said I'd come to my end with my boots on. Please take them off." Asa was crying now, pleading and sobbing.

Behind him his two confederates Con and Big Ned were taking their medicine without a whimper. But still Asa sobbed, "Take my shoes off. I beg of you, my last request."

"Take his shoes off," someone ordered. "Take all their shoes off. But keep the noose tight."

The desperadoes were swinging just a few inches off the ground, faces swelling and reddening. They were gasping for breath. Strangling by their own weight.

The posse was now bent on capturing Long Steve. "We can't let him get away."

One squad searched the railroad yards, another was assigned to guard the road to Fort Sanders, and still another to block the Overland Trail. In the freight yard, they found a train of boxcars and flats making up its string. The contents showed a dismal, disheveled array of human beings. Women (among them Diane Moore) gaudily clad, faces strained and full of fear. Men, paunchy of belly and sallow of skin, huddled together. Men who had but a short time ago, comprised Laramie City's tenderloin racketeers. The train moved out with its cargo—the riff-raff, the bawdy, the lawless. But Long Steve was not among them.

The sun was coming up over Sherman Hill, streaking the dawn with a new day. October 19. All night the squads had combed the town hunting Long Steve. They trailed him out to Fort Sanders and back to the rail yards. There they found him hiding in an abandoned shack. They brought him down Second Street and at the north end of the Railroad Hotel, where the street crossed the tracks, a telegraph pole beckoned menacingly.

The sun was well up now, and Long Steve, no longer the confident desperado, was cowering and pleading for his life.

"Let me take down the tracks for Omaha. Give me a sporting chance."

"You didn't give our citizens a sporting chance," they told him. "All summer long you've ruled. Now our people are going to have their say."

"We say put him in Hell!" was the answering cries.

Some of the men began adjusting the rope. "I'll assist him up the ladder," volunteered a citizen.

The face of Long Steve paled. "For God's sake, don't. Please, I beg of you."

The men paid no attention to his pleas. Again he begged,

Hanging of "Long Steve" Young, Laramie City, 1868.
Western History Reseach Center, University of Wyoming

"At least give me a drink of water." The rope began pulling him up. "Please, give me a drink of water."

"You can wait until you're in Hell and get your drink from the devil," someone shouted.

Higher went the rope, the men straining at the opposite end. Long Steve's eyes began bulging. Then the rope slipped and he abruptly dropped. A citizen rushed up the ladder, grabbed the hemp and gave it a ferocious jerk. This did the job. Long Steve swung, gasping and choking in the air. It was all over.

It was then Ed Ivinson came up with a stranger. "Boz," he said, "I want you to meet the Reverend Mr. Cook of Cheyenne. He came over to preach the sermon today. I invited him to see the hangings in the barn. Didn't expect to get a ring-side view on this, too."

The minister and Ivinson moved on down "B" Street, and another on-looker remarked, "He took it damned well for a preacher."

Boz, too, was moving away when he saw a boy. A small lad standing wide-eyed and open-mouthed, staring at the spectacle.

"Willie. Willie Owen," he put his hand on the youngster's shoulder. "What are you doing here?"

"I was just going to the store for Mother when I saw that man with the rope."

Boz delivered Willie to the Widow Montgomery, who lived nearby. Willie's eyes were popping, and his voice was cracking excitedly as he began telling the story to his mother and two sisters, Etta and Eva. "And a man came and took our pictures. And there was a preacher there . . ."

"Hush," said the aghast Mrs. Montgomery. "Don't you ever brag about being at that hanging. If you'd gone to the store this morning like I sent you, you'd never have been in that picture. Don't you ever let me catch you boasting about it again."

The street was deserted now. The town, too, was quiet—a sort of stupor had overcome it. A chill-nerve tightened silence.

Boz made his way back to the room behind the drugstore. He opened the window to let in some clean air, but instead the atmosphere was the breath of death. He'd felt it before, and he would never get used to it.

He went over to the table, pulled out a chair and sat down,

his face in his hands. They'd told him a committeeman had been killed by the outlaws, and the dance fiddler had been a victim, too. And there'd been some twenty others wounded. Yes, it was like Dave Cook said—the law of the frontier was shoot or be shot. The law of the gun, and sometimes the rope. It looked like it was the only way they'd let you survive in this wild land. Boz hoped at last the bloodletting was over.

He picked up a letter—another from Chief Dave Cook. Musgrove again. Disguised like an Indian, the horse thief had led his confederates in the dark of the night, whisked away over a hundred head of horses and mules from the Creighton brothers' camp near Elk Mountain.

"I'm putting Haskell in charge and deputizing you," Cook's message said.

That meant in the saddle again. Right now Boz wanted more than anything else, to bring Martha west and settle down. But he was duty bound and he knew what this assignment was: Musgrove, Duggan and Franklin.

Chapter 6

DEATH FOR THE HORSE THIEVES

It was no child's play, hunting down the kingpin of the horsethieves, Laurence Musgrove. A giant of a man, shrewd and impudent. Though uneducated, Musgrove was outwitting officers of several territories. About the time Chief of the Rocky Mountain Dectectives Dave Cook thought he had the bandit tracked down, he'd turn up on another border two hundred miles away. It was like a game of chess, trying to outguess the next move—Kansas, Nebraska, Texas, New Mexico, Colorado, Dakota or Utah.

At times, hot on his tracks, the posse would hit the corrals only to find Musgrove had beat them there, stolen a herd, sold it, swiped it back again, and made off to another region. It was a lucrative business for the outlaw ring, since mules and horses on the frontier were bringing a handsome price. Musgrove had been able to build up a formidable racket, but the detectives in the vast wilderness at last were making a dent in his operations.

Chief Cook told his network, "Musgrove's lieutenant, Jack Willetson, and two accomplices have been captured and lynched in New Mexico. The leaders are dwindling to a handful, but Musgrove is still at large. And he's dangerous. Killed two men in Nevada last year, and another in Wyoming while he was trader at Fort Halleck on the Overland. His headquarters now is a saloon on Denver's Holladay Street. Franklin and Duggan are teamed up with him, darting in and out everywhere."

Detective Cook put United States Marshal H. S. Haskell in command of the terrain of the Cache la Poudre. Boswell, his nose trained to flushing outlaws and Indians, with his volunteers was assigned to the northern border trails around Virginia Dale. Their chief told them "Could be you'll be in the saddle two days or two weeks. Pick your mounts knowing you may get sore in the tail bones."

Haskell and his posse rode all day across the trackless, brooding country. Just before sundown, they came upon fresh prints of a herd that had gone that way.

Lynching of the horsethief, Musgrove. *Contemporary drawing, courtesy Jeff Omodt*

Dusk was fast throwing a screen around them and the last crimson streaks in the sky splashed color on the low rock wall before them. They halted, and as they waited, there came to them the low whinnies of ponies, and in the next instant a man, a big man, stood in the opening of a cave-like gulch. He scanned the horizon, and after satisfying himself that there was no cause for alarm, he turned and retreated into the crevice.

"That's him, all right," Haskell whispered. "Barricaded in there, snug as a bug, and we can't get to him or the stock."

The lawmen decided they'd wait. "He can't stay in that dry wash forever. And he can't take the herd out over the back hills without us knowing it." the marshal said. "We'll wait him out if it takes all winter."

The hours wore on. It was a long and lonely vigil. But the outlaw did not appear again.

Morning came and went. And noon. The sun was sliding across the sky when the bandit showed up again. The posse now began closing in around him. But, protected by the rock walls, Musgrove faced his audience, guns in hands, he was the cunning confident desperado.

"And who might you be, may I ask?" the calm voice questioned.

"United States Marshal and deputies," Haskell answered. "We have reason to believe you have stolen property in your possession."

"You're barking up the wrong tree, Marshal. The animals I have corraled here, I bought with my hard-earned money." For a long moment his comtemplating glance moved from deputy to deputy. "But I'll play it fair. You can come into my corral here and have any stock you recognize." He was still fingering the triggers of his six-guns. "You can take same stock, but no more. Condition, of course, that I go free. You got no case against me."

One of the posse cautioned Haskell. "Could be he's taking us like gophers into a rattlesnake's hole."

But Haskell, unafraid, told the bandit, "We'll take you up on it, Musgrove."

Shoving one gun in the holster, the horse thief stepped aside, then sweeping his hat off his head, he bowed in mock politeness, "Age before beauty."

"Oh, no," Haskell told him, "we'll follow you."

As they entered the hide-out, the officers could see how invulnerable Musgrove was here. Stock securely staked and provisions stacked high against a granite ledge. He could last a month. All the while Haskell kept his gun leveled on Musgrove, while he ordered his deputies to pick out the known brands. There was quite a sizeable bunch. Some brands the peace officers were unsure of. They must leave these. And they must leave Musgrove, too. That had been the bargain. It was bitter gall that they had been duped into a truce.

The posse drove the herd out into the open. All the while Haskell kept Musgrove covered with his rifle. When the animals and the deputies were out of gunshot range and the outlaw was back in his hole, Haskell went aboard his mount and spurred him in the direction his men had gone. North.

They rode all day and camped at night. They had now reached the Wyoming border. Here Boswell and his men joined them. As they rode, Haskell had a hunch, "I have the feeling Musgrove is following us. He'll not be content with what we left him. It's not like the sonofagun to give up so easy. I'll wager he'll be along right soon and raid our herd."

So that night, the lawmen did not bother to conceal their camp smoke. They left the horse herd at the bottom of a slope, and then hid in the nearby brush and pines.

Darkness came. There were nervous nickers from the horses. Someone was moving among the animals. "Let's give him a little more time to unstake them," Haskell whispered.

As the herd was milling, the lawmen descended on the outlaw.

"Halt, Musgrove. In the name of the law, I demand you halt."

It was easy after that. The marshals had Musgrove trusseled up with a rope like a Christmas goose. "We'll take him in to Denver," they decided, "and turn him over to Cook."

There was great excitement in the Colorado city when the people learned that Musgrove had been caught and jailed. There were rumors, too, that Franklin and Duggan were on the outskirts of Denver planning to liberate their chief. In fact, they had Colorado in an uproar with their sudden spurts of hold-ups—frisking

46

and killing citizens—leaving a trail of blood that would have done credit to a Sioux chieftain.

The success of the Franklin and Duggan hold-ups led to open boldness. Late Friday night, November 20, they followed a prosperous-looking old gentleman down Lawrence Street. When he reached a deserted alley, they jumped him. With a pair of ugly revolvers aimed menacingly in his face, the old gent handed over his wallet as demanded.

Duggan said to Franklin, "Let's plant the damned old snoozer. What d'you say?" Franklin was willing.

Somehow, their captive was able to dissuade them. "I'm only a useless piece of humanity. Not worth your trouble."

Giving their victim a couple of vicious kicks in the butt and swearing at him, the thugs finally moved on their way, The next day, Franklin boldly called at the jailhouse to bolster the spirits of his leader, Laurence Musgrove. When the citizens learned of this, they began milling and talking in low whispers.

Yes, the luck of the horse thieves was running out. It began with the old gentleman they'd robbed. He was Judge Orson Brooks, and he'd sat on the bench in the trial of Duggan for the assault on the woman, Kitty Wells. Judge Brooks went at once to Dave Cook. "One of the twenty dollar bills Sam Duggan took off me was torn. I mended it with a piece of official paper from my office."

This was the clue Cook needed. He sent notices all over Denver and to surrounding towns to be on the lookout. By Sunday, Chief Cook was alerted that the men he wanted were in Golden. They'd been drinking there in a saloon and had paid with a torn bill. He must move quickly.

About two o'clock Sunday morning, November 22, the posse found brawny-muscled Ed Franklin in his underwear, sprawled full-length on his bed asleep in the Overland Hotel. The lawmen, carrying a lamp, saw that Franklin still bore the gunshot momentoes of his recent exploit in standing off Uncle Sam's soldiers near Fort Sanders.

Aroused by the officers' entry, Franklin grabbed his revolver from under his pillow. He fought like a wild-cat, but the odds were against him. Cook was not about to bet blood on even terms with an outlaw. "Shoot or be shot," and Franklin was dead.

There'd been a chase for Sam Duggan, but from his adjoining room, he'd heard the commotion and shots and had lit out in the dark of the night. He jumped a fence and hit for cover. Not, however, before a man named Hill was killed trying to stop him.

Musgrove, now in the Denver jail, brazen and defiant, was bragging how his comrades Franklin and Duggan would rescue him.

"You have no idea how up in arms and determined those Colorado citizens were," Cook later wrote. "Franklin was dead, but Sam Duggan was still on the loose."

Chief Dave Cook wanted to avoid any violence. But on Monday afternoon, it happened. A hundred or more good people—lawyers, doctors, business and professional men—marched on the jail. And no law officer dared stand in their way. It was the people's will. They'd had enough of Musgrove.

At the jailhouse, a speaker mounted on a stand, asked, "Shall Musgrove be taken out of jail and hanged?"

"Yes,' was the loud, answering chorus.

Musgrove, gazing from between the bars of the prison window in his husky bravado voice told them, "Come and get me. I'm ready."

Immediately the crowd broke down the door and the big bandit defiantly hurled a huge pine knot into the air, threatening any man who came close. His dark, serpentine eyes glared at the crowd.

He held them at bay, menacingly swinging the club at them. Then a gunshot rang out. A second. And a third. The bullets whizzed just over the head of the tall criminal. It was all up, and Musgrove knew it. He put down the pine weapon.

The procession headed him toward the Cherry Creek bridge. The pressure of the crowd pushed Musgrove to the front.

At last, the outlaw spoke. "If you are bent on murdering me, you will at least be men enough to permit me to write to my friends and tell them the shameful story of your conduct towards me."

So, in the middle of the bridge, using a railing Musgrove penned his final messages. When he had finished, a couple of men bound his legs together. The leader ordered: "Climb aboard the wagon. Driver, proceed to the noose waiting him."

Denver's Captain Scudder, religious and respected, tried to halt the hanging. But Musgrove nonchalantly was making a cigaret, turning the ends of the paper cooly and carefully over the tobacco crumbs. Then, with his hat pulled over his eyes, he sprang into the air to end it all. The same display of bravado he had shown all his life, he would carry with him to the grave.

"He was brave as all get-out," Dave Cook later told Boz. "As cool as a Mexican ranchero in his plaza on a summer evening. And his two death letters there on the bridge, he wrote with firmness and never once flinched. Here is a copy of the letter to his brother:

> 'Denver November 23rd, 1868 My Dear Brother I am to be hung today on false charges by a mob my children is in Napa Valley Cal—will you go and get them & take care of them for me godd knows that I am innocent pray for me but I was here when the mob took me. Brother goodby for Ever take care of my pore little children I remain your unfortunate brother
> good by
> L. H. Musgrove'

The other letter Cook asked Boz to deliver to Mary Musgrove in Cheyenne:

> "Denver, C.T.
> My Dear Wife—Before this reaches you I will be no more Mary I am as you know innocent of the charges made against me I do not know what they are agoing to hang me for unless it is because I am acquainted with Ed Franklin—godd will protect you I hope Good by for ever as ever yours sell what i have and keep it. L. H. Musgrove."

Boz read the story about the hanging in the Denver newspaper: "The people who assembled were good men . . . They were quiet and orderly, no shouting, no commotion—waiting to see the law executed upon one who had outraged them. They comprised a large part of the men of the city, and were not a crowd or a mob, but an assemblage of the people."

Now the determined and outraged populace of Denver had made up its mind to rid the country of Sam Duggan, too.

The horse was the economic lifeblood of the frontier. Stealing the herds was a profitable business for **Musgrove's syndicate. He** raided corrals from Texas to Utah.

Chapter 7

DUGGAN IS CAPTURED

When Sam Duggan escaped the lawmen in Golden, the Chief of Detectives Cook had reason to believe the bandit had hit back into the hills of Wyoming.

"Pick your posse," Cook told Boswell, "I'm counting on you to bring him in."

The Wyoming marshal was certain Duggan would give Laramie City a wide berth. "I have a hunch he'll circle and hit in a different direction. East out of our hills, and mebbe Nebraska."

Dawn fired the horizon and Boz headed his men that way. All morning they rode along a deserted mountain trail, hugging the foothills. They came upon an abandoned tie camp. They hit terrain where snow had fallen the night before.

"This'll help. See what I see? Tracks in the snow. Two horses went this way."

A few more miles and now they were in country surrounded by strange and misshapen juttings. "Natural Fort." Boz told his men. "I got a hunch."

Again he raised his hand for the men to halt. He'd go it alone. Get a closer look.

Boz had gone but a few yards, crowding the granite boulders for protection, when he saw a movement. There along the rock where water trickled downward to a patch of frost-nipped grass, Boz spotted something. Barely perceptible in the fringe of willows he saw two horses— a sorrel and a roan. His telescopic eyes missed nothing, told him the horses were sweat-caked and rope-tied. And not forty feet away was Natural Fort. He crawled stealthily toward the rock buttress.

The sun was glancing on the granite and that's why he didn't see the man moving toward the horse. But the man had seen Boz. And a gun roared. Boz ducked behind a boulder and out of old habit, his right hand moved and he was palming his gun. He was twirling the cylinder, checking the load when another bullet blasted, ricocheting the stone too close for comfort.

Then the lawman fired. The bullet thudded and the large man's gun went spinning like a quarter whirling into the air and out of reach. His hand was going down to his left hip, but Boz blazed again. For a moment the man seemed stunned.

In that instant, Boswell glided down the rock. "Hands up, Duggan. You're my prisoner."

"The hell with you," and the bandit was reaching again. But it was too late. The marshal had him covered. "One more move out of you," Boz told him, "and I'll blast you to hell!"

For a second, the two men eyed each other. The weak eyes of the desperado, bagged and tired. The steel-like, determined eyes of the lawman. Duggan knew he didn't have a chance.

"Drop your gun," Boz ordered. The revolver thudded to the ground.

That was when the second man appeared, coming from behind the rocky fort. A soldier in an unkempt, wrinkled blue uniform. Unarmed and surprised—an army deserter, Boz guessed—the fellow looked like he'd been caught sucking eggs. He ordered the man in a curt voice, "Hands up!"

Then the two deputies were on the scene. While the officers handcuffed Duggan, Boz kept his guns on both outlaws. "We'll take him in to Cheyenne, too," Boz told his men, motioning toward the deserter—"turn him over to Camp Carlin."

One of the deputies untied the horses and they all started back up the trail. Whenever Duggan balked, Boz shoved a gun barrel in his ribs. Up the slope and down the other side to their mounts.

News spread that Duggan had been captured and lodged in the Camp Carlin guardhouse. There was more milling around the street corners and men huddled together again, talking in low voices. Some wanted to lynch Duggan like the Denverites had done his confederate, Musgrove. Boz and Bill Kuykendall, probate judge, and D. J. Sweeney, sheriff, were able to talk the angry men out of it.

"Chief Cook will be in from Colorado himself to escort Duggan back to the Denver jail. We'd better have fast horses ready for him," Sheriff Sweeney decided.

They knew that the outraged populace of Denver had already made up its mind to make an example of Duggan by hanging him, too. "We'll let no villian escape. Duggan must follow in Musgrove's footsteps," the Coloradoans were saying.

The law officers were anxious to bring the offender to justice without violence, and so they must move fast. They could do double time by a private stage, hit Denver a full twelve hours before the regular run. They hired a driver they knew could handle the reins like a Roman chariJoteer, and they ordered a relay team to be ready half-way down the Colorado road. With their handcuffed prisoner, Cook and his deputy began their race. Boz and his posse would follow for security. The long whip snapped and the horses hooves drummed down the street and away. Mile on mile, they sped.

The hurried-up trip caught the Denverites off guard, but when the carriage passed the Carr House, almost at once people began pouring from all directions. And when the stage reached the courthouse, some five hundred men were gathered there.

"Plow through them," Cook ordered, and the horses snorted to a standstill in front of the jailhouse. The two-hundred-pound outlaw was trembling like an aspen leaf.

All over town the word had spread. "Duggan's in the county jail."

By four o'clock that afternoon both sides of Larimer and Fifteenth streets were lined with men, women and children. Some were already congregating out on Cherry Creek bridge.

Dusk came early, and many of the spectators figured darkness was no time for a hanging, and began leaving. It was then the officials decided to transfer the prisoner to the City jail on Front Street. As Duggan was being loaded into the express wagon, sharp whistles sounded. Someone was giving an alarm that the prisoner was being whisked away. Immediately there was an onrush of over a hundred armed men.

The irate Coloradoans took Sanford Duggan, outlaw, to Cherry Creek and hanged him to one of the cottonwood trees.

"Cherry Creek. Where those three cottonwoods are," the leader shouted.

In no time at all, they had the prisoner pinioned by several strong, armed men, and the carriage was being headed toward the bridge, where a rope was hastily looped. A couple of men lifted him into a spring wagon. Others held torch lights. The leader stepped up to the outlaw.

Duggan, chalky and shaking, begged, "A priest. Please send for a priest."

"We don't have time for dilly-dallying," one man said. "Get on with your confessions. Your minutes are numbered."

"I killed a man in the mountains, but it was self-defense. I have been a bad man, but nothing that deserves hanging. Please send for a priest, I beg of you." Duggan was alternatively sobbing and pleading. But the impassive vigilantes remained unmoved.

"Drive on," the posse's chief ordered, and the wagon which had served as the physical bulwark between life and eternity moved out from under Duggan. A coroner came. "Verdict: Death by exposure."

Sam Duggan, once marshal of Laramie City, and the last of the Musgrove ring, had been accounted for. With the leaders gone and the citizens bent on putting the fear of God into all Musgrove subordinates, it was apparent the lawless ring was broken for good.

It was sundown, late November, 1868. Already the winter winds were whining down from their glacier peaks. The snows of a long winter would soon be spiraling over this land and covering the trails.

And now Boz, relieved from his sleuthing duties, was to have a pleasant assignment. He was to help the committee with arrangements for Laramie City's first Christmas celebration. It was to be at the Railroad Hotel.

The planning chairman told him, "You're charged with the decorations. A big fir tree from the hills, and all the trimmings. Toys and treats for every kid, too. There'll be a program."

"And there'll be dining and dancing for us grown-ups," John Wanless put in. He winked at Boz. John knew about Martha. Martha would be coming into Laramie City Saturday on Number Three. And tomorrow Boz'd be going down to the freight office after the shining mahogany four-poster bed he'd had shipped west—the wedding gift they'd scarcely used.

Ah, at last Martha! Would she be changed? Nine long years. Yes, time certainly got away from a man!

Martha. He could see her—the way she looked sitting at the dresser on their wedding night, combing her long brown hair. Her waist as slim as a willow switch. Her grey eyes flecking blue and soft in the lamplight. Her voice, she was always singing. Had won some fame, too, back there in Elkhorn just this year—first one to sing Webster's and Bennett's new composition, *In The Sweet Bye and Bye,* at a concert!

Well, Laramie, wild and boisterous, could do with some singing. And some women, too—gentlewomen. He hoped Martha would make allowances for this crude, unpredictable frontier.

Archives-Western History Research Center, University of Wyoming

The "imposing hall of justice" where Boswell as Albany County's first sheriff, assembled the world's first female jury.

Chapter 8

"SHERIFF BOSWELL, SUMMON THE WOMEN JURORS"

It was remarkable how quickly Martha adapted to the harshness of the country. Right off she helped organize the Methodist choir and joined the Benefit Society "to dance the schoolhouse roof on." A church and a school. At last the marks of civilization in Laramie City.

And it was good to have her beside him, too, to share the honor of another appointment as sheriff. Charley Bradley was the representative to the Dakota Territory legislature and through his influence, the county, Albany, had been named for his native town in New York. But Bradley was sponsoring the likeable former wagon boss of Fort Sanders, John Connor, a Democrat, for county sheriff of the new territory, saying the Republican governor would have to go along with a Democrat legislature.

But many of the citizens were adamant. "We still need an experienced lawman. A man unafraid, who'll keep our county safe. There's only one man for that job!"

And Mel Brown who'd already had all the trouble he wanted as the town's plagued past mayor, spoke openly to Wyoming Territorial Governor Campbell. "Laramie City needs a stiff purgatory of law. Boswell has proved himself, earned his reputation as a criminal catcher and town tamer. Who else can keep the peace in a county that runs almost three hundred miles long, and that isn't even settled?"

White square-shaped building in center is schoolhouse. *Union Pacific collection*

Boswell attends the Golden Spike Ceremony, Meeting of the Rails, Union Pacific and Central Pacific, Promontary, Utah, May 10, 1869.

Union Pacific collection

There were happy and smiling faces that May day, 1869, when Boz raised his hand and took the oath as first sheriff of Albany County, Wyoming Territory. The ceremony was held in the small building pretentiously designated courthouse, but hardly aspiring to its dignified name. In the room assigned to its first peace officer, Martha hung the framed certificate of appointment signed by Wyoming Territory's first governor, John Campbell.

One of the honors coming to Boz that July was the assignment as marshal of the Golden Spike Driving celebration at Promontory, Utah, where the Union and Central Pacific railroads met.

Boswell hardly gave a thought then to the many historic episodes in which he had a part. One was an important date for this new territory. On December 10, 1869, the Territorial legislature passed, and Governor Campbell signed, a bill granting Wyoming women the right to vote and to hold office.

This was a big boost to a lawman's job. It was like Judge Howe said, "If women have their way, it'll be maternal force against brute force. And Wyoming women are casting off the shackles. I've witnessed among our frontier women a universal hopefulness and aspiration. It's good for the West."

Already the women had filed on town lots, and were going into business. Sarah Montgomery, a widow and stranded in the new town with her three young children, had opened her eating house "The Famous Restaurant." Hannah Murphy was running a hotel. "Aunt Mary" (as Catherine Erhardt was known) had filed on an acreage of land at the edge of town and had the first dairy and fresh egg business. Lucy Cordiner, with her precious sewing machine, made hats and dresses for the village matrons.

Yes, Boz was grateful to the town women for their part in keeping trouble down. But he knew, too, that to rid a wilderness all at once of its lawlessness was next to impossible. There was the time a horse thief stole Charlie Hutton's percherons. And he'd had to catch and lock up some robbers who'd broken into Gus and Charley Trabing's Cooper Creek store. Another time, the Arapahoes had gone on a rampage on the Overland Trail. He called on a squad of soldiers at Fort Sanders to help him herd the Indians into the guard house.

Boz opens the polling place election day, 1870, where for the first time in the world's history women had the vote.

"I've been on the outlaw trails so much, I've hardly had time to renew acquaintance with my wife," he said more than once.

The duration of his appointment to the office of sheriff was until the fall election when the voters would cast their ballots. His old adversary, John Connor, had announced his candidacy and he was posting placards from one end of the county to the other.

And this year, for the first time in history, Wyoming women were to vote. Because of this unprecedented event, the eyes of the world focused on Wyoming. Reporters and cartoonists arrived and it was predicted that the men would be protesting; that

Eliza Swain, first woman voter in the world, was escorted to the polls by Sheriff Boswell. *Archives-History Research Center, University of Wyoming*

there would be drunken brawls and squabbles. Boz stood by, ready to keep the peace.

Who would be the first woman to vote in a public election? It was decided that lovable, motherly Eliza Swain would have the honor. The sheriff was delegated to escort her, and to open the polling place. In a fresh apron over her gingham housedress, Mother Swain answered the early morning knock. "Just a minute please, Sheriff Boswell. I must get a pail to buy yeast at the bakeshop on my way home."

At the close of the polls that day, Boz reported to the town editor, "The men outdid themselves to be gentlemen. No liquor sold, no rudeness, no brawling, nor disorder, as the ladies all day went about the business of casting their votes."

And when the ballots were counted, Boz had once more defeated his persistent adversary. But the peace he'd hoped might come to Laramie City was still in the future. The town was running true to frontier form. Anytime, violence threatened to flare again.

The first evidence of this was the juries. They were becoming increasingly lax and indifferent. One by one he'd run down horse thieves and law breakers only to have the male juries turn them loose. By bribes or lack of evidence, too many of the desperadoes were being released to prey on society. "I'm about to the end of my rope bringing in these suspects. But I'll keep on rounding them up and trust we'll draw an honest jury to convict them," he told Judge Howe.

That's what he was thinking the night the air rang with an explosion of guns down at Pat Doran's Shamrock Hotel. Boz, buckling on his brace of pistol and summoning his deputies, lost no time getting to the scene.

Gunsmoke, thick and acrid, was pouring from the barroom. John Hocter was lying on the floor, dead. A dozen or so men stood around, silent and rebellious. Boz saw a stranger, a handsome grey-eyed man, standing spraddle-legged, his revolver still smoking.

"Who are you," Boz asked.

"Andy Howie. Just come to town."

"Who did the shooting?"

The dozen men remained glumly silent. Boz turned to

Howie. "What about this? Were you here when it happened?"

"I'd just gone upstairs to bed when a noise awoke me," Howie was talking fast now. "Still half asleep, I stole downstairs and in here. A pistol was leveled in my face and a voice said, 'I'm going to shoot you,' and the fellow shot twice. One bullet struck Hocter here, and the other grazed that guy over there."

Boz turned and saw Pat Doran slumped in a corner, groaning and holding his leg.

"I tell you it was stray bullets," Howie insisted.

Boz, scratching his chin, was thoughtful. This fellow Howie was talking too much for innocence. "Who did the shooting?" the lawman asked again. Once more he was answered by grim silence.

Boz motioned his deputies. "We'll take them all prisoners. March them out to Fort Sanders." Once the sheriff had them

Sheriff Boswell served subpoeny on Miss Eliza Stewart, first woman in the world to serve on a jury. Laramie City, 1870. *Condit collection*

locked inside the stone guardhouse, he told them, "You'll have the protection of the garrison against any mob violence. But only if the guilty one confesses."

It took a bit of prodding and persistence, but after a day or two Howie confessed. He had been the one who'd killed Hoctor. "But it was self defense, I tell you. Self defense."

No one believed Howie would be convicted in the upcoming trial. There'd been seven or eight culprits turned loose that spring—one right after another. Boz fretted and chafed that there'd be a return to the lawless days of '68.

But Judge Howe had an idea. He told Boz "If we can get women to serve on the jury, there'll be justice. The women of Laramie City are dead set against this law breaking."

And so for the first time in history, women were summoned. It was Boz appearing at the door of Laramie City's school teacher, handing her the summons: "Miss Eliza Stewart, you have the honor of being the first woman ever called upon to serve on a court jury."

The world's first woman jury, Laramie City, 1870. The cartoonist depicted it as all-female, but it comprised members of both sexes. Here, the caricaturist insinuates that Sheriff Boswell is "riding herd" on his wards.
Frank Leslie's Illustrated

Besides Miss Stewart, Boz called also Mrs. Amelia Hatcher, Mrs. Sarah Pease, Mrs. G. F. Hilton, Mrs. Mary Mackel and Mrs. Agnes Baker. Mrs. Baker was excused, but the others served.

Now, Case Number Twenty-six, Wyoming Territory versus Andrew Howie—charge murder, loomed conspicuously on the court docket. The prisoner, eyeing the women in the jury box,

Martha Symons Boies Atkinson, came to Laramie City when it was a tent town. She served as the first woman bailiff for the historic Women's Jury, 1870. *Wyoming Historical Department*

frowned. It was then the defendant's attorney, Stephen Downey, moved to quash the panel on the grounds of it not being male. Chief Justice Howe, with Associate Justice J. W. Kingham concurring, overruled him.

Word spread fast that women were actually sitting in judgment in Laramie City. Eastern reporters and cartoonists and photographers flocked to the courthouse, poking sly jokes at the female jurists. The ladies steadfastly refused to pose for pictures. The cartoonists portrayed them in all sorts of absurd situations. One ridiculous caricature depicted them holding crying babies on their laps and soothing them, "Baby, Baby, Don't get in a fury. Your mama's gone to sit on the jury." Others made snide remarks about the men and women of the jury being housed in one bedroom.

Judge Howe promptly squelched that opinion. "Sheriff Boswell, you will appoint a woman bailiff." Boz selected Mrs. Martha Symons Boies Atkinson for the honor. "I also have engaged two rooms at the Railroad Hotel. One for the ladies, and one for the gentlemen of the jury. At the door of each there will also be a bailiff."

When Mrs. Boies was announced as bailiff, some man noticing Howie's nervousness jokingly said, "Howie might well be fidgety. The bailiff's husband running a funeral parlor and her driving the hearse."

The court was called to order and Boz heard for the first time in history, a judge address the jury: "Ladies and Gentlemen of the Jury." Then the presiding judge spoke to the women: "The eyes of the world are upon you. You shall not be driven by sneers, jeers and insults of a laughing crowd from the temple of justice as your sisters have from some of the medical colleges of the land. The strong hand of the law shall protect you. You are pioneers serving in a movement to test your power and protect yourselves from the evils of a lawless civilization."

For two days and two nights, the jury heard the case of Howie amid much activity. It was reported that the wife of the minister prayed. Some men openly predicted the oratory would sway the women to acquittal. And then the West received the surprise of its life. The jury found Andrew Howie guilty.

For three weeks, the mixed jury was in session hearing

cases. Boz gratefully observed the determined women convicting murderers, cattle and horse thieves and rustlers. They found saloon keepers who kept their business open on the Sabbath guilty.

But the woman jury did not turn Laramie City over night into a peaceful and law abiding town. By fall and into the winter months, Boz was in the saddle again, rounding up, arresting and bringing to justice the lawless. In November, his friends John Meldrum and L. D. Pease came into the sheriff's office to report three valuable horses stolen.

For some time, Boz had had his eye on a pair of hard lookers hanging out at the Shady Nook Saloon. He strolled over to see if they were still there. No one had seen them for a couple of nights. Boz jumped into his saddle and headed old George to Ingersoll's.

"They came in yesterday," the stableman told him, "but left right after getting their saddles. Rode out of town heading West."

And so Boz was on the trail again. "Alive or dead," he told Meldrum and Pease, he'd bring in the horse thieves. If humanly possible, he would catch them and force surrender. Dead—he'd bring them in that way—if there was no other alternative.

The weather was nippy and the mountain air smelled of frost and snow. Hugging the old Overland, he rode across the swells of the Laramie plains. Still following it, he skirted Elk Mountain, heading toward the Red Desert. He was certain he was on the right track, because every now and then he came upon fresh ashes of a campfire. Hoof prints, too, of horses.

"I followed them clear into Utah," Boz later reported. "Once I had them in shooting range, but they discovered me and gave spur to their mounts. Then one night, I got ahead of them, riding around by a side trail. When they came jogging, they got the surprise greeting of their lives. They were looking into my doublebarrel shotgun!"

Still covering the outlaws, he ordered them to unbuckle their holster belts. He cowed them into putting handcuffs on each other. Then with the stolen stock and his captives, he headed back for Laramie City. It meant constant vigilance, hobbling the horses each night and sleeping with one eye open. "Once I awoke just in time to catch Oakes and Miller moving, crouching toward me."

" 'Get back there,' I told them. 'Don't you ever do that again or I'll blow your heads off!' "

He brought them into Laramie City and jailed them. The county commissioners were high in their praise of the lawman, and in board meeting, voted "The fees and expenses incurred by Sheriff Boswell in the case of the Territory against Oakes and Miller amounting to the sum of $120 be promptly payed."

As far as the reward money went, Boz would have none of it. "I was just performing my duty," he told Meldrum and Pease.

Chapter 9

A COLD BLOODED KILLING

It was 1870 and Boz was still a member of the Rocky Mountain Detective Association, as well as being sheriff of Albany county, when a Mr. Maxwell of Denver sought his help.

A little over a hundred miles to the West in Wyoming Territory, the Union Pacific had been building its line through the country in 1868. It was here at Fort Steele John Kelly, a contractor, was in charge of the construction work. He had hired the sixteen-year-old son of Mr. Maxwell to work as night herder of the stock being used. In a fit of anger, Kelly had shot down and killed the boy, Charley.

The facts of the murder were well known to lawmen of the West. It was a cruel, sadistic slaying. That early summer of 1868 young, likeable Charley Maxwell had come from Colorado with his parents' consent, and his fine pony to work for Kelly. From the beginning, the contractor held out the youth's pay checks, saying "I'll give you your money when the season ends—when you're ready to go back home."

Charley's father sent the boy a minor's release, but Kelly ignored it. To add further insult, the contractor worked the kid night after night without relief.

"Some men'll stoop to anything to make money," fellow workmen said, "Kelly's that kind."

One night a bunch of Indians stole Charley's prized pony.

His fellow-workers took up a collection and bought him another. At the end of summer, Charley went to Kelly's office in the warehouse and told his boss, "Pa says my school is starting, so I must go home, Mr. Kelly. Could I please have my wages?"

The burly contractor, his feet propped on a desk, turned a pair of surly eyes on the youth. After a deliberate minute of annoyed silence, Kelly opened a drawer and began counting out bills. Before handing the money to Charley, the contractor told him, "I've deducted the price of that new pony from your wages. Here's what's left."

"But Mr. Kelly," Charley reminded him, "It wasn't your money that went for that horse. It was my friends who pitched in and bought him for me. It was their money, not yours."

"Why, you little bastard!" Kelly, red-faced and angry exploded as he stood up, towering above the lad. "Get this straight. This is all the money you have coming. And now you get out of here. And you stay out!"

Some of the employees loitering outside the warehouse overheard Kelly and the kid. Some of them were Charley's benefactors who'd bought the horse for him. The men cursed under their breath. But Kelly was their boss, too, and more than one of them already had cause to fear Kelly's violent tantrums. One, however, did advise Charley: "Don't be a sucker. That's your money. He signed the pay contract with your Pa to turn it over to him. Before you leave, you go again and tell him you want what's due you."

Fort Steele, Wyoming Territory, where Jack Kelly killed young Charley Maxwell in 1868. *Union Pacific collection*

Fort Steele was a cluster of log buildings, tents and barracks huddled in a scattered shape. There were freight wagons pointing westward bound for the grading camps and the bridge work ahead. Construction engines funneled up black smoke. As Charley strapped his bedroll to his saddle, Freighter Reed with his string of six mules called to him, " More rain today, Charley. But you can travel east with General Gibbon's troopers. At least as far as Virginia Dale."

Charley called back, "Thanks, Mr. Reed, and goodbye. See you next summer, mebbe Weber Canyon."

And then Charley saw his boss, Kelly, stomping out of the warehouse and slamming the door behind him. The contractor was heading into the Fort's little commissary bank. That was Charley's mistake—following Kelly, and trying again to collect wages due him.

The clerks inside told how Kelly turned from the cage and began stuffing greenbacks into his pockets. How Charley faced him, "I came to remind you about the money you owe me, Mr. Kelly." How Kelly, his anger showing in his face, it getting as red as a fire engine, and his eyes as wild as a tiger, spilled his wrath in words, "Why, you dirty little bastard. I'll teach you to ask me for money," and he stomped out the door, slamming it. You could hear, they said, his cussing as he went pounding down the rough board walk. You could see the look on the boy's face that he knew now he'd never collect the money. He started walking slowly toward the hitching rack where he'd reined his pony.

That was when the loitering men saw Kelly coming back out of the warehouse. He had a rifle across his shoulder. They relaxed their fear, however when the contractor walked to the opposite side of the road. But their relief was short lived. Kelly was directly opposite the hitching rack toward which Charley was walking. Before they knew it, they were caught as spectators in a horror drama.

They heard Kelly shout, "Halt, kid. I say halt." Kelly was kneeling now, leaning against the wheel of a wagon, the rifle pointed directly at the boy. In the next instant, they heard a deafening blast. There was the acrid smell of gun powder and Charley falling.

Writhing in pain, half rising on his elbow, the boy cried, "Oh, Mr. Kelly, you have shot me."

The Irishman had not moved. Freighters and timbermen and railroaders who had been sauntering up and down the board walk stopped in their tracks. Too stunned to move, they saw Kelly stand up, his carbine crouched in his arms. The look of cruelty on his face. It all happened so fast, they were too stupefied to act, as they watched the big Irishman cross the street. Kelly reached the youth and towered above him—the men heard in the deathlike silence, Charley's plaintive pleading, "Please, let me live. I won't bother you again. I promise, Mr. Kelly."

Then they heard the savage bellowing voice of the contractor, "No, you won't ever bother me again. And you'll play hell asking me for money in a public place. I'll see to that." The muzzle was against Charley's ear now. Half his head blown off. Someone took a shot then, a freighter maybe, revived from his shocked paralysis, but Kelly was running and the bullet barely licked a crease across Kelly's face. Then another shot, its lead thudding in the dust behind the killer. Kelly had too much distance. Now he was inside his warehouse. Its door closed.

"Let's go after him. Let's lynch him," the men were huddling in circles. Another said, "Quick, let's get the constable."

A burly timberman, his boots sinking in the mud, walked over to the dead boy. As he gazed down, he took off his hat and, with the back of his hand, wiped his eyes.

The marshal came then. The men motioned in the direction Kelly had disappeared.

"If you don't get him, we will," they told the officer.

True, Kelly was their boss, but this cold-blooded murder was too much to stomach.

Kelly was locked up in the Fort Steele guardhouse. But shackles and bars were no deterrent to the fiend. One night he overpowered the prison guard and escaped. It was the same in Omaha where they tracked him down, arrested and imprisoned him. Only there he used his money to bribe his freedom from the watchman.

The killer had been at large two years when Charley Maxwell's father came to Boz with information from Chief Dave Cook. Kelly was in jail in Council Bluffs, Iowa, and the Rocky

Mountain Detective chief recommended Boswell as the man to bring the desperate murderer to justice back in Wyoming. It was a dangerous mission.

Boz slipped the warrant for Kelly's arrest in his pocket and kissed Martha goodbye. He would travel by train to Council Bluffs. He'd get his man and be back in a few days.

That was his plan when he left Laramie City. But carrying it out was another story. He was dealing with a hardened killer, and a clever one at that!

The first jolt came when Boz went into the marshal's office at Council Bluffs. Yes, a few weeks back, the officer told him, they'd arrested Jack Kelly. But he'd flown the coop on them. Shot his way out of jail. No, they had no trace of him now.

This was a real set-back for Boz, but he was determined to capture Kelly. He'd not turn back now. He'd given his word to Dave and Mr. Maxwell. He'd get their man if humanly possible. Charley Maxwell's murder must be avenged.

But he'd come to a dead end. As he moved around town, he kept his eyes and ears open to local going-ons. That was how he learned the Burlington Railway was extending its line into the timbered and knoll-rolling terrain to the east. He went down to talk to the rail superintendent.

"I'm looking for a contractor named Kelly," Boz told the official, "They tell me he's employed someplace along your road. Have you any knowledge of him?"

The superintendent leaned back in his chair and thought a minute. Yes, he was sure the company had given the job to a big Irishman—a contract for the stretch of grade about three miles out of Red Oak in Montgomery County.

"I have some business with him," Boz told the official. "How do I get to Red Oak?"

"The nearest railhead, Pacific Junction, is about forty miles from Red Oak. A wagon road connects it now."

With a timetable under his arm, Boz left the office. From the map he would study the terrain, get acquainted with the lay of the land. He'd also learn the train schedules—once he arrested Kelly, he'd need to make fast time—get him aboard a westbound. And he'd enlist the aid of the Montgomery County sheriff.

Heading back to the hotel, Boz decided to get a good night's sleep. In the morning he'd hit for Red Oak where he'd begin a hunt for a man who'd killed a boy back in Wyoming.

Next day Boz arrived in Red Oak and went immediately to the courthouse. Introducing himself to the local sheriff, Boz showed him the warrant for Kelly's arrest. The Iowa lawman volunteered: "I'll help you any way I can. We'd better take out after him bright and early."

Before dawn the two sheriffs were hitching a team and climbing into a rig. They would follow the river route as it wound in and out of the draws.

It was late spring and the road was rough and rutted. The pace was slow, and as the morning sun came up both men scanned the terrain as they moved over it. They kept their eyes alert to any movement along the fresh cut banks. Suddenly, on the opposite side of the grade, the figure of a big, burly Irishman appeared. "That's him, all right," Boz said. "That's our man."

Almost at the same instant, Kelly saw the approaching wagon. He stopped, shading his eyes with his hand.

"We're in luck," the Red Oak sheriff told Boz, "We've caught him alone—away from his camp and crew."

Kelly, the crook of his elbow raised to shade his eyes from the sudden penetrating sunup, watched the approach of the carriage. Then abruptly he turned. He was almost in a run now as he moved in the opposite direction. That was when Boz called, "Just a minute, Mr. Kelly." But the fugitive continued in his flight. The Iowa lawman flicked the reins and their team spurted forward. Kelly broke into a fast run, cutting across the open terrain. Boz, his eyes scanning the country, saw Kelly was heading for the dark object in the field about a half mile away. It was a span of horses hitched to a wagon.

"Stop, Kelly. I order you. Stop!" Boz called. But Kelly's reply was an added spurt, his fast tracking legs taking him into a ravine.

"We'll lose him," Boz said, "He's taking a short cut and this wagon can't make it. We've got to catch him. And on foot."

Quickly the lawmen jumped from the carriage, and began racing. They were gaining on the man. Boz called again, ordering Kelly to halt. But their man was in a dead panting run. Boz's hand moved for the grip of his pistol. He called again, "Halt. Kelly, I say halt." But Kelly kept going. Boz, his eyes fixed on his target, tripped the trigger and sent a bullet after the fleeing man. It kicked up the dust behind his target. "Damn you, Kelly, if you don't stop now, I will shoot to kill," the sheriff shouted.

Boz was an expert marksman, but he had only revolvers. The distance between him and his man was lengthening. The odds of hitting Kelly were against him. Nevertheless, he had to chance it. Squatting and resting his six-gun on his knee, he took deliberate aim. He fired.

There was the crack of the sixshooter and Kelly screamed. He catapulted on his back, his hand clutching his stomach. "My God. You've got me. Don't shoot again. I surrender. Do you hear me, I surrender!" His hands were up in the air now.

Still covering their man, the officers moved in. Kelly was lying on his back. Boz, wary that his victim might be feigning, came forward cautiously, his gun leveled at the man.

"No show of blood," the other officer told Boz and knelt, unbuttoning Kelly's shirt. Boz kept his gun leveled on their captive. "He doesn't seem to be seriously hurt. The lead seems to have made a clean bore—out through the navel, probably."

Kelly, still lying flat, began cursing vehemently. "You goddamed sonsabitches! Taking advantage of me unarmed! Murdering me in cold blood."

"You're under arrest," Boz quietly told him. "I guess you know why without me telling you. But just in case you need reminding—it's for the murder of Charley Maxwell." Kelly's face blanched. The officers carefully lifted him, taking his arms and supporting him between them. They began retracing their steps toward the rig.

Despite Kelly's fuming and swearing, the Montgomery County sheriff counted off the distance Boz's bullet had traveled to hit its target. "Man, what a shot. You dropped him at two hundred twenty yards. And with a six-shooter!"

Their progress toward the carriage was slower now. They were taking pains with their prisoner, stopping every now and then for him to get his wind. They had almost reached the rig when they heard a great clamor of shouts. Boz, looking back to the road bed, saw a mob—about sixty men swarming toward them. They were coming faster now, gathering sticks and stones as they came.

"We'd better get to the horses and fast," Boz told his companion. The burden of the wounded Kelly suddenly became dead weight. Purposely he was slowing them, while the ranting, yelling men gained ground.

Above the shouting, Boz heard a loud, shrill voice, "You're not taking my brother with you! Do you hear? You're not taking Jack." The chorus of rushing men came louder and closer. "We say you're not taking Jack. We'll kill you if you hoist him into that wagon.'

"Keep your distance," the cool-voiced Boz warned them. "We came here for this murderer. He's under arrest and we're taking him back with us." His revolver was leveled menacingly at the sea of grizzled dirt-smudged faces. "Don't any of you come any closer. Get up in that buggy, Kelly."

"I can't. You've shot me. I can't stand up," Kelly was whimpering now.

Boz, his revolver still trained on the angry excited mob, ordered his fellow lawman, "Shoot him. If he doesn't climb up into that wagon at once, shoot him."

The order had its effect. Kelly meekly climbed into the vehicle. Almost at the same instant, the two officers jumped into the carriage, covering the cursing, milling hoodlums, with their guns. A flick of the reins. "Giddap. Giddap," Boz commanded, and the horses, as if sensing the perilous predicament, took off. The air behind them was filled with blasphemy and howls of vengeance. Boz stood facing them, steadying himself against the seat back as his companion handled the reins.

"Get up the dust," Boz said, "It's our only hope. We've got to outrun them. We'll stop first in Red Oaks." The driver whipped the team to a fast trot.

As the vehicle jolted over the road, their prisoner moaned and groaned that they were killing him. Boz, his eyes still strained on the disappearing objects of howling humanity, his Colt still pointed, said "We'll have a doctor look you over when we get in town."

"My brother will get you for this," Kelly threatened grimly. "Him and his friends won't let you get away with this." Then he lapsed into sullen silence.

76

The rattle of wheels continued, and the horses' tails whipped in the morning breeze. The lawmen were driving for their lives, heading toward Red Oaks with their prisoner.

A contemporary drawing – author's collection

Mike Kelly and his frenzied mob tried to prevent the lawmen from loading their prisoner on the Westbound train.

Chapter 10

BOZ GETS HIS MAN

The sun was hanging behind layers of white clouds. It had not yet reached midsky when the two peace officers, with their prisoner, came down Red Oak's Main street and pulled to a stop in front of a physician's office. Boz jumped down and the two men helped their prisoner to the sidewalk.

A small man with a goatee, carrying a pill bag, came out of the door.

"Wait, Doc," the Iowa sheriff called. "We've got a man here shot up. We need your help."

The medico helped the officers get Kelly out of the wagon and inside. The captive, sour as a green apple, was bent over, holding his stomach. In no time, the man of medicine had him in the second room and on the table. The lawmen stood nearby. They were taking no chances of their man escaping now.

"He's been dangerously wounded," the physician said. "His chances of pulling through are about two to one."

"We'd hoped to get him to Pacific Junction," Boz confided.

"Might as well try it. His chances of living are so slim anyhow that further travel won't lessen them. Here, I'll wash and dress the wound."

But Kelly was floundering and raving again. "I won't go with them. They can't make me go." Ignoring his curses, the officers held him while the doctor probed the wound. As they waited for the bandaging, Boz took the timetable from his pocket and examined it.

"If we hurry, we can still catch the westbound out of the Junction."

"Go ahead," the doctor said. "Make a bed for him in the buckboard."

Kelly was still protesting, but the men ignored him. They loaded him onto a bed of straw in the spring-wagon, exchanged their team for the fastest horses available, and hit out for Pacific Junction, thirty miles away.

Over the rough roads, down the steep gullies, around the sudden curves they went. "Every minute counts," Boz calculated.

At last they passed the half-way distance and the going got easier. Kelly had settled into a grim and sullen silence. The sheriffs relaxed.

But their relief was short-lived. As they jogged along over a corduroy road through heavily timbered bottom land, Boz's trained ears heard a clatter of hooves. To the left of them he saw a cloud of dust heading their way. Kelly's crew!

"Looks as though they're plumb determined," Boz told his companion.

There were about twenty men in all. Some were mounted on mules and some on work plugs. In a flash, Boz saw they were armed with shotguns, shovels, pitchforks. They were galloping fullspeed. And Mike Kelly was in command. They'd taken a short cut through which no buckboard could go. Sudden death stared the law officers in the face.

The team had slowed to a walk. "I guess we might as well face the music. Pull the horses up. It's them or us."

The mob was still coming at them. "Get ready," Boz directed his ally. Then in a loud voice so the leader would hear, he said, "Sheriff, keep your pistol on Jack Kelly's head. If he or his friends get too rambunctious, let him have it."

Boz, his guns pointed at the crowd, jumped from the buggy. With cool, steady eyes he gazed at Mike Kelly.

Their captive's brother was advancing toward the buckboard. "You thought you'd make suckers out of us, did yah? Well, the table's turned."

Boz raised his six-shooter. "Halt," he ordered. "Don't you come one step nearer." When Mike paid no attention, but defiantly motioned his backers to advance, Boz's hand moved to the grip of his pistol and his eyes were fierce, his voice cold: "Move one inch nearer and I'll shoot you in your tracks."

The warning had its effect. The attackers drew the reins of their plugs. The stillness was that of Death.

"Now what do you want?" Boz asked in a matter-of-fact voice.

"You know what we want. We came for Jack, and we intend to take him back with us."

"Oh, you do, eh! Come on, then. But if you do try it, you'll be taking him back to the coroner."

The group shifted uneasily. They saw the muzzle of the cocked revolver, its bead on their leader. They saw, too, the muzzle of a second gun in the other lawman's hand. It needed only the squeeze of a trigger to send Jack Kelly to Kingdom-come.

It was the prisoner speaking now. His voice trembling and unsteady as it rose on the afternoon air. "Boys, listen to me. For God's sake, don't come any closer. Mike, do you hear me? Listen and do as I say. The odds are against me. They will kill me."

"That's right," Boz told them. "If you come any closer, Jack Kelly is a goner. And before we're through, we'll make a dozen corpses of you."

There was a huddled conference. Jack Kelly was still pleading, "These officers mean it. They'll plug me. Go back. Do as the sheriffs say."

"All right, Jack. If you say it's best," it was Mike talking. In another minute he turned and ordered his men to retreat. Reluctantly, they pointed their mounts in the opposite direction. Ranting and cursing, they moved away. Boz stood rigidly watching them disappear through the oaks and off into the horizon. Then he climbed to the wagon seat.

"Fifteen miles yet to Pacific Junction," he looked at his watch. "If we whip the horses to a run, we can still make the train."

The wheels rattled on again. Ten, five, then two miles. Kelly's whimpering accompanied the commands of "Giddap. Giddap." They were almost at the edge of town and the overhanging tree limbs shaded them from view as they neared the business intersection of Pacific. There was a penetrating whistle from a train on the early evening air.

Boswell was detailed by Rocky Mountain Detective Chief Dave Cook to track down the Fort Steele killer, Jack Kelly, and bring him to justice.

And that was when Boz saw in the thinning twilight, a strange congregation. He heard, too, the clatter of hooves and the snorting of animals.

"It's them again," Boz said. "Better detour."

The Iowa officer knew the Junction like a book. "We'll make for the hotel. We're in luck—they haven't spotted us yet." He was pulling hard on the ribbons to turn the horses into the winding side street down a lane of trees.

They reached the hotel and it was quiet. The officers hitch-racked their sweat-caked and quivering horses. Jumping to the sidewalk, they helped their prisoner down.

Inside Boz walked up to the desk, his badge in plain sight. "We got a reason to press a team like that," he told the hosteler. "We'd appreciate your man taking care of the horses. And we need a room. Right away."

Barricading themselves in their room, the officers got their captive into bed. Barely in time, too, for a great commotion was going on downstairs.

"All we want is my brother, Jack Kelly," Mike was demanding of the proprietor. "Tell them to turn him over and we'll leave."

Their arguments did not persuade the manager. So up the stairs they came, stomping, swearing and shouting. Boz could hear them kicking at the door, trying to break it down. They were still storming when the town marshal arrived with his rein-forcements.

It took a little time, but these officers finally routed the would-be rescuers. Boz went to the window. He heard an engine's melancholy whistle and saw its headlight on the station. He had the feeble hope that the train might be delayed and they could yet make it.

Except for the grind of wheels coming to a stop, it was quiet outside. The hotel was backed up to the depot with a long, wide boardwalk connecting it. Helped by glimmering rays from the headlight, Boz was able to make out a platform which was really a plank passage over a marshlike pond. He heard the engine's whistle again. Then he saw it was a freight train pulling into the station. Still he was willing to chance it. If at all possible, he would board it with his prisoner.

"I'll see you loaded," the Red Oaks sheriff told him, "Then I'll check on the horses and spend the night here."

"I'll help, too," the town marshal assured Boz.

The two Iowa officers took the captive by the arm. Boz, with his revolvers cocked, brought up the rear. The minute the freight pulled to a stop, the hosteler opened the rear door. They walked out.

A bunch of disheveled, belligerent townsmen had joined the mob. With Mike Kelly as leader, they were bunched in knots flanking the platform. There was a dead silence as the officers, their badges and guns in full view, advanced. As they passed the first group, it stirred and shifted uneasily. Then a wild yell ripped the early evening air. Mike Kelly, his eyes menacing and savage, lifted a hand. The platform became a formidable human wall, preventing further advance by the lawmen and their prisoner.

Someone yelled, "You haven't got a chance. Not a chance against us!"

Boz punched his guns harder into the ribs of his prisoner. His ally officers' hands were on the butts of their revolvers.

"Gangway," Boz ordered. "Gangway."

There was an instant's hesitation and then the wall of men divided, leaving an aisle for passage. "It was like the Red Sea of old rolling back," Boz later told Dave Cook.

Directly in front of them was a freight car, its doors pushed open. Still pressing through the crowd, walking briskly and dragging Kelly as they went, the lawmen headed for it.

They still had about ten feet to go when someone jeered. Another man picked up a piece of cord wood and hurled it, hitting Boz in the back.

Like a bolt of lightning, Laramie City's sheriff turned. "Crack. Crack." His guns were smoking and the bullets whizzed just above the heads of his tormentors. They saw he had them covered, and they saw he meant business. Frightened, they now moved back, jostling and shoving. Then some of them broke into a retreating run. More than one in haste to quit the scene got spilled off the platform. Into the soupy pond they fell.

Others, like a bunch of wild trail steers, began stampeding. A great many disappeared running into the adjoining cornfield. Even in its seriousness, it was a ludicrous scene.

But Mike Kelly didn't run. And a small bunch of the daring toughs stood by him. They surrounded him protectively as he jumped on a fence post. Above the melee, Mike had his gun trained on Boz. But he wasn't fast enough.

Boz, with a long smileless look, tripped the trigger and sent a bullet plowing. With a wild scream, Mike grabbed his thigh. The smell of gun powder had an anaesthetical effect on the mob. There was not a voice raised or gun fired.

But there were still a few hoodlums standing near the tracks. As the officers briskly headed Jack Kelly toward the freight car, these ruffians made a dash to scramble aboard ahead of the lawmen. Reinforced by some yardmen, the brakies with billy clubs beat them off.

At last Boz had his captive safely inside the car. There was a shrill whistle and the Iowa peace officers jumped off. The train moved out, and the surly, grumbling killer, Jack Kelly, was at last in the custody of Boz and the trainmen.

There was no doubt that the violent affray had been hard on the wounded man. Boz worried about his prisoner's condition. He told the conductor, "He seems serious. I'd better stop off with him in Council Bluffs and have a doctor look him over."

The trainman wired ahead and when they pulled into the Bluffs, a surgeon and ambulance were waiting. In the jail cell, the specialist gave Kelly a thorough check up.

"To proceed with him in his condition is endangering his life. But given a little rest and care, he'll be all right again."

While the prisoner was on the mend, Boz kept his watchdog eye on him. Despite his vigilance, the Wyoming sheriff was taken by complete surprise a couple of nights later when a big ruckus sounded outside and a mob stormed the jailhouse. Through some devious means, Jack Kelly had managed to slip a letter out and get it mailed.

There was another big gunfight—the law against the lawless. Again the assailants were driven back. "It looks as though I'll have to blow a hole through your guts before you leave me alone," Boz told Mike Kelly.

When next the prisoner's brother struck, it was with a more subtle weapon—soft soaping Boz and offering a big bribe. He would make it worth the Laramie lawman's while—$40,000-if he'd just be off guard on a certain night.

Boz appeared to mull this over, "That's a lot of money. I'll have to think about it. Come back a little later and I'll give you my answer."

By thus stalling, Boz was assured of no immediate jail storming. In the interval, he hoped to get his captive across the Missouri. But he must have the physician's diagnosis again—was his prisoner recovered enough to move? He was.

With the doctor's assurance, Boz loaded his prisoner aboard the Union Pacific passenger train heading for Nebraska. Slowly, but steadily, he was getting the criminal back to the scene of his crime.

But troubles still plagued Boz. It took only a day for Mike Kelly to discover he'd been duped. Like a bloodhound sniffing the scent, he was fast on their tracks, pursuing and catching up with them.

Boz and his captive were registered at the Cozzens House in Omaha when Mike connived to get a note to his brother.

But N. K. took no chances. He hired a husky fellow named Day to ride herd on Jack while he attended to necessary details at the depot. Before Boz went out, he saw Kelly was undressed and in bed.

Boz had barely been gone a half hour when Jack Kelly began tossing and groaning. "I've got Goddamned cramps," he moaned. "I've got to get to the privy."

This meant taking Kelly to the outhouse which was in the back yard. Day'd have to put the prisoner's shoes back on him. As he reached down under the cot to get them, Kelly snatched the guard's revolver.

"Go to sleep, Sheriff," and Kelly's gun boomed.

Day screamed. He went down with his hands clutching his chest.

In the next moment, Kelly was up and heading for the door. Although bleeding badly, the deputy managed to get to his feet and rush after his prisoner. Kelly was unlocking the door. Before he had it opened, Day was on him.

There was a desperate struggle, but the guard got his hands free and with knotted fists, plowed into Kelly, battering him hard.

The shot and the shouting and the smell of acrid gunpowder brought the hotel guests on the run.

"Be careful," Day shouted. "He's got a gun." A couple of big men grabbed Kelly and held his arms. The revolver fell to the floor where Day picked it up.

By this time, the hotel clerk came running into the room. The bellboy was right behind him. "Quick," the clerk ordered the boy, "Go after Boswell. He's at the railroad station."

Boz was just turning away from the ticket office when the bellhop came panting, and Boz knew something had gone wrong. He lost no time getting back to the hotel.

To avoid any curious guests who might be loitering in the lobby, the peace officer circled around to the back door. In his haste, he almost bumped into something.

It was a carriage drawn up and a horse rein-tied to the fence. There was a great commotion, a pushing, shoving mob was storming the rear door. But blocking their way was the hotel proprietor, Mr. Ramsey. In the lamplight, Boz could see the old gentleman, like a Roman gladiator, standing at the stair bottom, holding the crowd at bay with his gleaming sabre.

To get inside, Boz jumped through an open window. Now he, too, was facing the agitators, his gun barrels menacingly trained at the cursing men. They had no doubt about it—Boz and Ramsey meant business. Abruptly the routed beseigers turned and fled.

That night the sheriff escorted Jack Kelly to the county jail for safe keeping. And he was relieved to learn that Guard Day's wound was not serious. But if Boz thought that was the end of his troubles, he was wrong.

The lawman was still fearful that Mike Kelly would keep trying some trickery and so he employed a railroader, Tom McCarthy, to pose as a trouble shooter and keep him informed of anything suspicious.

In this way, Boz learned of the secret obstruction which went up six miles west of Omaha. The railroad company was now alarmed and immediately took Mike Kelly and his conspirators into custody.

At last Boz, with the killer Jack Kelly, was rolling over six hundred miles of prairie lands, headed for Wyoming, a trip of two days and a night which required the lawman's constant vigilance.

When the train pulled into Laramie City, the town's marshal, and Deputy Sheriff Tom Dayton, with his men, were at the station. The tale of Kelly's terrible crime and the troubles of his capture had reached the territory. Jack Kelly was handcuffed and escorted out to Fort Sanders' prison to await trial.

Chapter 11

ROUNDING UP MORE OUTLAWS!

They were still living in the rooms behind the drugstore when New Year, 1871, dawned.

"There's talk of a new courthouse," Boz told his wife as they were eating supper that January night. "There'll be living quarters in it. But government building is awfully slow. Not sure just how long it'll be."

"I'll wait," Martha said. These rooms had been home ever since she came to Laramie City. And although Boz had suggested several times that she might like a cottage in the new residential area to the east, she'd been content to live on Second. And it was less lonely than being in a house.

Sometimes Boz was gone for days at a time and here on Second, she had many women neighbors—wives and mothers living in the rear or above the store buildings. And they were real thoughtful of her, too, when Boz was away hunting down law breakers. They were always including her on picnics to Hutton Grove and Dingley Dell and to Sunday afternoon concerts when the Infantry Band at Fort Sanders held open house.

To be sure, she worried a good deal about him; the dangerous assignments he undertook. She supposed she never would quit that inner trembling as Boz so frequently kissed her goodby to head out alone after vicious desperadoes. But it was rewarding to hear the high praises for his efficient enforcement of the law. She was aware that his name was becoming famous throughout the Territory. "A capacity for cool judgment and hard courage," Governor Campbell had praised her husband.

And Boz was finally selling the Cheyenne drugstore. "Putting all my eggs in one basket in Laramie City," he told Martha.

Western History Center, University of Wyoming
Albany County, 1871. Here Sheriff Boswell confined many prisoners in the basement hoosegow.

"I'll close the deal this Saturday. How would you like to go along to Cheyenne? Judge and Mrs. Jones have asked us to be their guests."

That is how they happened to be in the Capitol City the night Jack Watkins went on his shooting spree. Judge Jones and Boz were strolling downtown when a man came rushing up.

"Judge, it's that drunk Jack Watkins again. He's shooting the lights out of everywhere. Got the marshal cornered and scared witless. You'd better stop it or Watkins'll kill him."

"Come along, Boz. You're duty bound to assist a fellow officer, you know. Watkins is a good shot and I hear our marshal's a poor dodger. And," Judge Jones added, "come to think about it, this man Watkins is from your county. Let's go."

"But I never laid eyes on Watkins in my life. Besides, you've forgotten—I'm out of my jurisdiction. I'm sheriff of Albany County."

"I'll fix that," Judge Jones answered quietly. To Boz's astonishment, he heard the Judge deputizing him. "You are now a United States deputy marshal assigned to arrest Jack Watkins."

They headed toward Sixteenth Street. As they approached a side avenue, they heard a great commotion. It was a sight to behold—whisky bottles flying, shouts of alarm answered by "Whoopee!! Hooray for Hell!" And a couple of men surrounded by a crowd stood facing each other, revolvers drawn.

"He's going to do the sheriff in," someone said.

"Watkins," the authoritative voice of Boz came through the mob. The two assailants wheeled around to hear who was interfering. "Go get him," Judge Jones urged Boz.

Boz unafraid, pushed through the mob. The dark-hatted man pointed a six-gun. But the Laramie lawman grabbed him and relieved him of his revolvers. "You're under arrest."

The other assailant bowed, turned and walked away.

"Now you listen to me, Watkins," Boz was saying when an uproar came from the crowd. "Not him. Not him." The crowd was shouting. "He's our deputy sheriff. The other fellow is your man. The one going down the street. The one you let get away. There he goes, Jack Watkins, your man."

"He's heading for the Shannon Saloon. He'll be shooting the lights out of it next."

Sheepishly, Boz realized he'd made a mistake. Embarrassed, he turned and rushed after Watkins. The renegade heard the racing footsteps and wheeled to face his pursuer, his sixguns drawn.

"I wouldn't fire them if I were you." Boz spoke calmly. "There are five hundred men here. Armed men. If you shoot, they'll riddle you."

"Who in the hell are you?" Watkins asked.

"Boswell, deputy United States marshal. And you, Jack Watkins, are under arrest."

"So you're Boswell! Well, I'll be damned. I've heard about you. And I like your nerve. Now, if you will protect me from this mob, I'll submit to arrest."

"You'll not be molested," Boz assured him. "Just hand over your guns. You'll be safe in custody."

They had proceeded but a short distance in the direction of the jail when Boz heard the crowd following, clamoring and shouting angrily. He turned to face the sea of belligerent faces. He saw one man with a coil of hemp.

In a chorus, they demanded, "Turn him over. He's our prisoner. We want Watkins. We'll teach him to shoot up our town. Give him to us."

Boz didn't bat an eye as he stared them down. "Not one foot closer," he said tersely. Then he handed the revolvers back to Watkins."If any man of you moves a step nearer, we'll put some bullets through you. Jack Watkins is a prisoner of the law and I'm locking him up. Now move back. Everyone of you. Get going or we'll blow your damned heads off."

"That's Boswell," the leader said. "Surest shot in the country." "I don't want my craw filled with lead," another spoke up. "Let's get out of his way, men."

It was easy after that. Locking Jack Watkins up in the county jail. "You have my respect," Watkins told his rescuer. "Some lawmen would have been interested only in making a name for themselves. You have my admiration."

The Boswells returned to Laramie City in time for the dedication of the new courthouse. The whole town turned out and a picnic lunch was spread on the courthouse yard between Fifth and Sixth. Speeches were delivered and United States Marshal Church Howe presented a handsome clock for the splendid court chamber.

"When the jail cells are finished, we'll really have our hands full," Boz told his deputy. "With the new counties, Uinta and Carbon, having no place for prisoners, Bill Hinton and Isaac Lowry will be lodging their lawbreakers in my hotel for safe keeping. That is, if I'm re-elected."

And Martha, too, was busy. She and Nancy Fillmore organized a community choir. They sang for benefits. And even for Fiddler Bill's funeral, when he died from wounds in a drunken brawl. "They called us and we rode in a black hack out where he was buried in a pauper's plot of the city graveyard."

And now, before they knew it, another election day had rolled around. Boz, nominated by popular acclaim, won hands down that November, 1872.

But he didn't move Martha into the courthouse apartment provided for the county sheriff. With the sheepish grin of a man about to divulge a secret, Boz told the commissioners he was to become a family man. But his jailer, Bramel, would like the courthouse accommodations and his wife would cook for the prisoners.

It was five days before Christmas and Boz was bringing home toys. A cradle and a high chair, too. On the twentieth, the little blonde daughter was born. Her delivery was not an easy one and according to the family doctor, Martha endured a suffering known as milk fever. But despite the painful post-birth affliction, Martha, with her courageous spirit, made no complaints and was soon up and about.

With the dawning of the new year, there were other responsibilities heaped on Boz. Laramie was to get the new Territorial penitentiary and until the buildings were up, he was charged with the keeping of the prisoners. He was also custodian of the jailbirds from the two other counties.

It was spring before he moved into the courthouse. His cousin, Emily Richardson from New Hampshire, was coming West. She would help out "boarding the prisoners."

Living in the county apartment gave Boz a chance to rebuild his drugstore on Second Street. A lot of other merchants followed his example, putting up more permanent structures.

In fact, it looked as though Laramie City was about to settle down. Churches going up. And schools. And a little hospital

Wyoming Penitentiary located across the Laramie River. For a time in the 1870's Boswell was warden. *Western History Center, University of Wyoming*

down by the tracks where Martha helped in emergencies. The frontier doctors never had enough nurses.

The Dawson brothers were doing a bustling business sending timber down the river. The army's sawmill was going full blast adding more barracks to Fort Sanders, and supplying the town with lumber. Laramie City had water, too, thanks to John Wanless, fort sutler, and Morgan Knadler, who'd brought in the garrison's dredge machinery to dig ditches up and down the streets. The citizens observed Arbor Day by planting trees.

Martha said it was hard getting used to the trenches through which the aqua flowed. And, more than one lady, stepping from a carriage after a night's sociable, splashed into a newly plowed irrigation ditch.

"We sink barrels and let the water settle in them for household use," Martha wrote her mother, "And do you know I'm going to have to hire a new cook? Our Emily has fallen in love with Deputy Caleb Jones. Right under our noses, too."

The hour glass of 1872 and '73 moved on. A good friend, Ned Spicer, was appointed warden of the penitentiary. This gave the sheriff more time with his family.

Of course, he was still often in the saddle, hunting down some renegade. The ruffians weren't letting a peace officer get rusty. Yet, compared to those first years, it was like Sunday School.

Then one day, the county commissioners called a meeting and asked Boz to sit in. The courthouse's roof was on, but the officials were edgy about funds to pay off the bonds. Boz was taken by surprise when the chairman told him they expected him to make calls over the county to collect taxes.

"Some of these dead beats won't come in and pay up. You'll have to go after them. Or take their stock in payment."

Boz was chagrinned by this assignment. It was a big country running from Colorado to Montana, ranches miles apart, hard country to get over. But mostly, he hated dunning these pioneers for delinquent payments.

"It's a mighty unpleasant pastime," he confided to Martha. "If that's what it's going to be like from now on being sheriff, I'd rather not be it."

He got his rathers. At the 1874 election Boz went down in

defeat at the polls. John Brophy was willing to ride in a buckboard journeying over county trails hundreds of miles, and harass the delinquents. In fact, Brophy preferred the roving assignments to hunting down gunslingers.

But Boz was not to be unharnessed just yet. He barely got his family settled back in the quarters behind the drugstore when the mayor and councilmen came calling.

"There's a lot of riffraff running around loose that needs locking up. You helped clean this town up once. We want you to keep it that way. We want you for city marshal."

As town marshal Boz locked Calamity Jane in the klink more than once.
McMicken collection, University of Wyoming

That night Boz confided in Martha, "Being town constable will not be as demanding as county sheriff."

But already he was speaking out of turn. He was hardly in office before a bunch of thieves stole a herd of horses from Spicer. And George Fox lost a dray team. And Martha Jane Cannery, alias Calamity Jane, came into Laramie City whooping it up, cracking her bull whip in the saloons and bellying up to the bars. Boz, more than once, had to confine her to the klink.

The soldiers, too, fancied themselves scrappers, and the railroaders resenting this, took Saturday nights to turn the Shady Nook Inn on South Third into a brawling place. "Send for Boz," was the cry when trouble brewed. Then periodically, Jack Watkins went on a toot.

It was a May day in 1875 when a county official came running for Boz.

"Jack Watkins has shot up Brophy and his deputy. We need you, quick."

It seemed that Watkins from his ranch at Wyoming Station, and his hired hand Sam Rogers, had walked into the sheriff's office to get a replevin for a stolen horse. Watkins was well known by the officers for his lawlessness, although since his spree and encounter with Boswell in Cheyenne, he had been living quietly on his ranch. Deputy Larry Fee came in while Watkins was waiting for the replevin. Seeing Jack, the officer (Fee) mistook Watkins' intention. Without any questions, he began writing out a warrant for Watkins' arrest.

Rogers, standing by, became greatly excited by the turn of events, "This arrest is uncalled for." When Fee paid no attention, Rogers, quick as a flash, went for his gun. Fee grabbed it. The two men began scuffling. Watkins tried unsuccessfully to calm his hired hand.

That was when Sheriff Brophy heard the commotion and came into the room. Immediately the lawman recognized Watkins and, acquainted with his drunken sprees too, made a lunge for him. But Jack Watkins was a match for any lawman. Without batting an eye, he freed himself, backed off, drew his revolver and fired. The bullet grazed Brophy's side. Before Fee could get into action, Watkins aimed and sent a slug of lead boring into the deputy's right leg. With both officers down, Watkins lost no time hightailing it for "A" Street and the Excelsior Stable. In his flight, he bumped into a hayrack and splashed into the water tank. But even soaked and delayed, he was intent on a get-away. He rushed for the stall and a saddle for his sorrel.

Back at the courthouse, the wounded sheriff sent a messenger scurrying for Boswell. In ten minutes Boz, who was also a United States deputy marshal, was riding out of Laramie hot on Watkins' trail. Into the north and west country all afternoon he followed the outlaw's tracks.

Just as the sun went down on the jagged hills, Boz closed in on his quarry. He took a long shot and dropped the fugitive, but in an instant, Watkins was in the saddle again and gone.

Surprise attack and Hold-up on a Cheyenne-Deadwood Stagecoach.
Frank Leslie's Illustrated

"He escaped out of the country," Boz reported, "probably badly wounded."

For a long time, "Reward" and "Wanted" posters were out for the outlaw. Apparently he'd had enough of Laramie City, its sheriff and its town marshal. He never returned.

But now another threat to law and order on the frontier loomed ominously. It came about by the discovery of gold in the Dakota Black Hills and the resultant boom. Into the country flocked bands of road agents fathered by Doc Middleton, waylaying the stages and holding up the treasure coaches. Everywhere in Denver, Cheyenne, Laramie City, Deadwood, men gathering heard of the robberies and murders. An air of fear and unrest again gripped the West.

The Indians, too, were on the prod, led by Crazy Horse and Man Afraid and the medicine of Sitting Bull. Martha, meeting with the Methodist Ladies Aid, heard the women fretting, "Will we never have peace? Must our husbands always be ready with their rifles on a moment's notice?"

And right in the midst of the new surge of lawlessness, the government decided to lay out a route, a shortcut, from Laramie City to the Black Hills via Fort Laramie. Boz, W. O. Owen and James Ingersoll were commissioned to survey it. They would commence right away, January, 1876.

"It'll be a tedious and lonely job. We'll be away for weeks." Boz told Martha. "Wouldn't you enjoy a visit back to Elkhorn? You and Minnie?"

So Boz put his wife and little three-year-old daughter and Aunt Tye, too, on the train, kissing them goodbye and assuring them the road agents and the red men wanted none of his tough old scalp.

The early months of the new year were busy ones for him— pegstaking a road in the wilderness, chasing lurking bandits and scouting for Indians on the rampage. Martha was not yet home and so that spring, he signed up with his old commander, General Crook for the Big Horn Expedition. Crazy Horse and Sitting Bull and Man Afraid were beating their war drums again.

In Laramie City that summer there was an air of lawlessness and unrest. Sheriff Brophy was still hobbling about and the citizens were edgy about unsavory characters hanging around.

Boz barely got his family settled from the trip back home when Marshal Balcombe pressed him into service rounding up some of the hoodlums. "You're still the best detective the West has seen. And I hear Jack McCall has drifted into town from the Black Hills. Keep an eye on him."

"You mean that guy that calls himself Jack Sutherland, swaggering around here drinking and boasting? The fellow with the broken nose and crossed eyes?"

"The same," Balcombe told the lawman, "There's something about him bears watching. There's those that still swear he killed Wild Bill Hickok."

Boz had seen Sutherland several times. Sandy-haired and mustached and always bragging. "Yes," Boz told Balcombe, "he's been in and out of the saloons a lot. He's now crying that someone robbed him of seven hundred dollars and threatens he's layin' for the thief."

It was a few days later, in August, Boz encountered McCall (or Sutherland, as he preferred to be called) in Crout's Saloon. "He was drunk and George Shingle and I sat down at the bar beside him," Boz later told Sheriff Dayton. "I couldn't help notice as he talked of Wild Bill how his hand clutched his shirt. He got a wild gleam in those crossed eyes, too. When he began waving his revolver butts, I up and arrested him."

Boz notified Balcombe, "Dayton and I've got Jack McCall locked up. Mebbe you better come get him. If I'm not wrong, Dakota'll be requisitioning him. There's enough witnesses to his confession here, the way he's been bragging about it all over town."

When Editor Hayford heard McCall was locked up in jail, he called on him. "He got his deserving's, Wild Bill did," McCall told the *Sentinel* Editor. "He killed my brother back in Hayes, Kansas. I didn't forget that. I evened the score with the sonofabitch. After I shot him, I stood facing that crowd in the Cricket Saloon. I'd had a quarrel with Wild Bill the day before the shooting about some gold dust he robbed me of. Between three and four o'clock that afternoon, I went into the saloon where Wild Bill and some others were playing poker. Thinking of my dead brother, I just up and shot Bill, the bullet going through his ear. I aimed my gun at the fellow sitting alongside, but the damned cylinder wouldn't turn.

"So I ran out the door where I had my horse tied. But the cinch was loose and the saddle slipped. That left me in the midst of an excited mob. I saw I couldn't make my getaway, so I gave myself up. Lucky for me while I was lodged in the jail, a Mexican came riding down the gulch with an Indian's head hoisted in the air. That diverted everybody until they had time to cool off. Twenty-five armed men guarded me until they could give me a regular trial." As McCall talked to the journalist, his face was twitching, his eyes were wild and he kept nervously fingering his throat. "But not a single person there could prove I'd killed Wild Bill. They hadn't seen it and they couldn't point their fingers at me."

"Well, they can now, McCall," Boz told the criminal. "George Shingle tells me he saw the shooting. You slipping in the door shooting Bill in the back. Shingle was right there in that saloon that afternoon when it happened."

Balcombe came to pick up McCall that day, and Boz told him, "Wild Bill may have been a good-for-nothing, but he didn't deserve a dog's death."

Of course the Laramie citizens followed the fate of McCall. Writing to a pal, Paddy Doyle, January 13, 1877, McCall blamed his troubles on liquor. His letter was published in the Territorial newspapers:

> "Dear friend: I have got my trial and will be hung Thursday the first day of March. You asked me if you thought it would pay to go to the hills in the spring. I think it would if you save your money and above all things let whiskey alone. So farewell forever on this earth.
> Yours, Jack McCall."

It is true that Boz aided the capture of McCall and that he had a hand in a number of other arrests which curbed lawlessness in the city that year.

"I had Jessie James locked up, too," he told the *Sentinel* editor. "But I didn't recognize him then. His cousin, Mrs. Bramel, was our jailer's wife and Jessie escaped." Only later did Boz recognize Jessie when he saw the likeness on a reward poster.

With an excellent record as town marshal, Boz had every reason to assume he'd continue in the job.

But when he learned that his old political antagonist, John Connor, had inched out another trustee for mayor, Boz was certain he could kiss his job as constable goodbye. ·

Boz was right. Mayer Connor appointed John Colford as marshal. Boz was offered the office of assessor, but he declined it.

"Smoke of a Forty-five." Charles Russell painting.

Chapter 12

NO LAW NORTH OF LARAMIE CITY

New Year, 1877, and Boz out of office, both city and county, hung his coat on the wall peg.

"I've worn the badge so long I seem kinda naked without it," he confided to Martha. "I feel like an eagle whose wings have been clipped."

Martha, her eyes on Boz, sensed something of his inner conflict—that he was apprehensive that his years as a law enforcer were behind him; that the epoch of a frontier singed with gunpowder and risk and violence was drawing to a close; that men of his breed were destined for a place on the shelf.

The Boswells moved back to their rooms on Second Street and the townspeople were going ahead with plans for a big January ball to be staged at the courthouse. The corridors were gaily decorated. A good band was hired. Officers and their ladies from the Fort came. Couples waltzed and quadrilled in long, flowing gowns and Sunday-best suits. Young ladies smiled into the eyes of the blue uniformed officers as the lads filled out their programs. In the halls, long tables were piled high with turkeys and hams and five-tiered cakes.

And while all these festivities were in full swing upstairs, Richard Duff, confined in the basement cell for horse stealing, continued to chink away with a case knife at the frozen underground. By February third, he had a tunnel twelve feet long. Out he crawled to freedom.

"That ground as hard as hell, too," John Donnellan told Boz, "Frozen since last November."

A little later, five more prisoners escaped. The newspaper publisher made no bones about the situation. "Our new sheriff is a first rate hand to catch criminals, but has awful bad luck keeping them."

And then another prisoner broke for freedom, seriously wounding Jailor Bruyn. "These jail breaks, three or four of them in as many months, is quite monotonous," wrote Editor Hayford. "We hear a great deal of grumbling among the people."

"If you'd replace those damned wooden cells. They're not strong enough to keep a cat inside," a citizen told Commissioner Jim McGibbon.

In no time, another escapee sawed himself out of his confines, but his attorney Charles Bramel, hearing the commotion in the building at the time, grabbed a rifle and got the escapee cornered. They told it all over town—how the prisoner quipped, "It's the first time my attorney has taken much interest in me!"

Things were going from bad to worse. The outlaw Bevins sawed his way to fresh air. The new York House was broken into and Bill Crout's safe at the Frontier spirited away.

Next there was a break-in at Henrietta Bath's boarding house, and Aunt Mary Erhardt had two crocks of dimes stolen. Then began a worried rumor going around that the town's new lawman had been lead poisoned.

However, the *Sentinel* editor, though not void of humor, cleared this up. "It is reported erroneously that Sheriff Nottage was shot in the parade ground yesterday."

Now the long riding riff-raff began coming into the Territory. This outlaw pack spread the word "No law north of Laramie City." Lured into Wyoming by the fat pickings from the Black Hills stage line, an aggressive and persistent criminal combine swooped down on the land. These men of deadly trades rode North by West along a secret outlaw trail.

Operating from a hidden valley guarded by the gaunt peaks of the Rockies they came. Among the outlaws were the James brothers, the Daltons, the Youngers, Dutch Charley and Big Nose George Parrotte. On the run from other states where law officers had murder warrants and rewards out for them, they now rendezvoused in Wyoming.

Far to the north of Laramie City, but still a part of Albany

County, the Trabings had a half dozen stores dotting the wilderness. These were the objects of continual break-ins and robberies. Gus wrote the county commissioners, "The government has sure forgotten us up here. We need protection. They're robbing us blind."

The town and county officers complained they couldn't get the commissioners to increase their forces. Marshal John Colford, in disgust, resigned, and Larry Fee, still limping and carrying a bullet in his leg from Jack Watkins' gun, agreed to replace him. But the lawlessness was more than anyone had bargained for.

In June came the news of a robbery of the Black Hills stage coach. "While all of us—the driver and passengers—were eating breakfast at Day's ranch on the Wyoming cut-off route," Laramie City's Mrs. Tonn told, "two masked men climbed on the boot and made away with the treasure box." Next flashed the distressing news of the Hat Creek holdup. And on its heels a Sioux ambush in which the cousin of Boz, Jab Simpson, was killed.

Almost at the same time, the Trabing brothers posted a $500 reward for apprehension of the robbers who had broken in their store at Medicine Bow.

From the top of a long grade flanked by wild plum thickets they said these bandits sprang, surrounding a coach marked for a robbery.

"Hands up," the band's leader ordered, his gun trained on the driver. Another would grab the reins of the lead team. They had the passengers at their mercy.

"Get down off that box and keep your hands up. Turn your back to me."

"Shoot the first sonofabitch who turns around or lowers his hand. Search the passengers. Here, that big bearded guy. I saw him stow away $500 in his shirt in Deadwood two days ago."

Or maybe it would be the shotgun guard they'd order, "Keep your nose to the front or I'll blow the top of your head off." If a man presumed to fidget or move his hand downward, a blast from a rifle put the finishing touches to him.

The newspaper editor Hayford complained continuously about how the county commissioners were bent on collecting taxes while the highway men operated without interference.

Then a particularly fiendish crime was committed on one of

the Deadwood stages. It was Marshal T. Jeff Carr of Cheyenne calling for help.

He came to Boz. "A desperate character is at large. He's been seen riding north of Laramie City, we think headed for Canada by way of Jackson Hole country. If he reaches the Hole, our chances for capture are lost. It's a nesting place for outlaws. You're familiar with all those hidden rincons and you're still a United States marshal. I'm commissioning you to bring the outlaw in."

"It's rough country," Boz told his superior, "And it'll be hard riding. But I'm at your command."

"I'll need evidence that you get your man," Marshal Carr told his deputy. "Bring him in, dead or alive."

Once more, Boz kissed Martha and his little daughter goodby. He didn't know how long he'd be away, but on his reliable mount, Prince, and with some hard tack in the saddle bag, he was off, heading northward.

United States Marshal T. Jeff Carr, Cheyenne, assigns Boswell to a dangerous mission. *Wyoming Historical Department*

Through pathless terrain, he rode. There were tracks of timber wolves and mountain lions. There were fresh horse prints, too, so Boz had the hunch he was gaining on his quarry.

On the fourth morning, he came to the sod-roofed log cabin of an old acquaintance, a former Canadian wolfer called Frenchy.

He stood at the door awaiting an answer to his knock. When Frenchy opened it, the lawman took in at once that the grizzled Canadian had played host to someone at breakfast—a table with dirty dishes for two.

Yes, the wolfer told Boz, a man had stopped for the night. "I let him stay. In fact, he left just about two hours ago. This man was a mean looker and I have a wife and family and I'd like to see them again. He said he'd not harm me if he could have a bed for the night."

"If you'd exchange horses with me for a fresh one, I'll be on my way," Boz told his host.

"You're taking a big chance, Marshal. Like I said, this fellow sounded mean and you may find yourself suddenly looking down his gun barrel."

"That's a chance I'm duty-bound to take," Boz said.

The wolfer scratched his matted hair. "Then I think I'll go with you. He's a real bad hombre and believe me, you're asking for sure death to follow him alone."

Boz assured his host he had plenty of ammunition and he'd take no foolish chances.

Shaking his head, Frenchy went out to the corral to bridle a fresh mount for the lawman. Boz was soon in the saddle and saying goodby to Frenchy.

He avoided open terrain by taking short cuts, and thus getting ahead of his prey. He saw the desperado round a bend, so Boz dismounted. But the movement attracted the attention of the hunted man. As fast as the wind he, too, was out of the saddle and behind a big rock.

It was a battle of wits—one man trying to outmaneuver the other. Once Boz removed his grey Stetson, put it on a stick and hoisted it in plain view, hoping to draw fire and thus disclose the exact whereabouts of his man. But the ruse didn't work. Still patiently he waited.

Now and then Boz sensed the man was peering cautiously from behind the protective boulder. He began debating what next he could do to attract and outwit the villian. He'd like to end the silent feud in favor of the law. But how?

Suddenly, out of the deathlike stillness, there came the rip of a rifle report. It was from the north, and beyond the enemy. Boz, peering from his cover, saw in the distance a man standing, motioning the marshal to join him.

Then he recognized Frenchy—the wolfer, and Prince, too, close by. The Laramie lawman left his covert, but still rode with caution. He was wary even yet for the wolfer might be the outlaw's ally. The two had spent last night together and the marshal could not know what confidences might have been exchanged.

Prince whinnied as Boz approached. Frenchy called, "It's all right. He'll not be holding up Uncle Sam's mail coaches nor killing lawmen ever again."

They were standing over the fugitive now, and Boz saw Frenchy had made a clean shot, boring a bullet through the villian's head. The dead man was a sight to see—hogshead chest, small eyes, bearded face.

"Good and proper evidence," Boz's superior, T. Jeff Carr, had ordered. How could he manage transporting the corpse all the miles back to civilization? He was still pondering the problem when Frenchy suggested, "His head'll do."

Marshal Carr had no doubt about the fate of the wanted criminal when Boz returned and personally presented to his chief the decapitated head as "good and satisfactory evidence."

Chapter 13

THE BANDITS GROW BOLD

Boz said afterward that Diane Moore passing through town the summer of '78 was a bad omen. He'd never forget the days back in '68 when she and her man Asa Moore would lure men inside their dives. And if he hadn't been warned, he'd never suspected her for that kind—her honey blonde hair and her innocent, soft blue eyes.

And now, even though she'd married again and had a bunch of small kids, and was headed for the Oregon country, she brought back thoughts of that other year. That wild, unruly one in Laramie City.

"You'd never know her, Boz," Aunt Mary Erhardt said, "But she did seem rather nervous sitting up there in that spring wagon alongside this new husband. They camped in the willow clump here on my land. And bought eggs and milk this morning. She's older and settled, and wearing gingham, and her hair more like dried straw stringing from her poke bonnet."

Editor Hayford spoke up, "I interviewed her. She could only exclaim about how Laramie City had changed. And how it had grown and how quiet it was. Not one word about the man she once dealt faro for. Nor did she ask to visit his grave out there in potter's plot."

Talk about Diane always made Boz nervous. It brought to mind the nights when the Bosses Five had set out to get him. A marked man, and Diane the Delilah.

Well, she was a changed woman, now, according to Hayford. And Boz wished her luck in Oregon—a homesteader's wife.

Only her passing through was a bad omen. Now and then he was assailed with these strange, disconnected presciences.

For Boz was aware that a great many strangers were hitting the town. You couldn't help noticing them. It was claimed that the Dalton brothers had filed on a lot at 517 South Seventh. At least their names were on the deed. And the Youngers had been seen drifting in and out of Laramie City. Badmen, all of them, who'd stop at nothing. And suspicious characters were said to be sneaking in and out of Rock Creek, Medicine Bow and Fetterman.

All spring this year of 1878, settlers from the north country came in to complain about robbers holding up their ranches, the outposts and stage stations. The Trabings, whose commissaries were frequent bait for the bandits, in desperation wrote their lawmaker, Stephen Downey, in Washington: "Unless something is done to strike terror into these outlaws, our holdings are doomed."

So bold had become the operations of the criminal combines that Union Pacific Superintendent Ed Dickinson petitioned Congress: "I consider it dangerous to run a train on the line." But Washington remained indifferent.

And so the long riding riff-raff gathered—operating from their hidden valleys and secret chasms. And each successful holdup spurred on their boldness.

In Canon Springs, there were several stickups. At Rocky Gulch, at Hat Creek, at Fetterman, at Crazy Creek, at Medicine Bow, at Trabing City, at Brown's Six Mile, at Fort McKinney.

Gus Trabing, from the north country, wired Governor Hoyt a third time: "These assaults are getting monotonous. Our storekeepers' lives are in hourly jeopardy."

The Territory could not help but be concerned with affairs when Mrs. Dickinson and Mrs. Brockway of Laramie City described their escapade shared by some hundred other train passengers. "We were well out of Rawlins when we were aroused from sleep by two masked bandits. Four men fired shots to let us know they meant business. Conductor Mills and W. C. Ramsey grabbed two of them by the throats. But the wretches' accomplices quickly clobbered the railroaders with the butts of their revolvers."

The renegades not only robbed the travelers, but also rifled the express car before pulling the cord and jumping from the train. Carbon County Sheriff Lowry and his deputy, Jim Rankin, and Marshals Bill Daley and Gustave Schnitzer, organized a posse.

"We were close on their tracks," Rankin reported, "but we lost their traces. Then we spotted a raft floating down the Bow and figured they'd taken to water to decoy us."

All up and down the Union Pacific towns there came stories that queer-looking strangers were milling around, some wearing

Reward Poster for the James Brothers' gang. Using aliases these desperadoes terrorized the frontier. *Union Pacific collection*

REWARD

$15,000 REWARD
FRANK JAMES
DEAD or ALIVE

moth-eaten silk hats, others carrying sawed-off shotguns. And all with good horses.

"Good horses and cheap," Boz told Superintendent Dickinson, "because you can bet your life on it they're stolen."

Sometime after this, the Union Pacific propositioned Boz to serve as special detective. One night while riding the Nebraska to Laramie City line, he saw a suspicious character board the train. He noted the stranger at times flashing light signals from his window.

NOTICE!

$5,000 REWARD

will be paid for the capture of

COLE YOUNGER

MEMBER OF THE NOTORIOUS JAMES BAND!

Keeping him under surveillance, Boz became certain the man was sending messages to some secret ally on the plains. When the train pulled into Laramie City, the lawman arrested the fellow and locked him up, telling Fee he'd bear watching. Later, the officer found their prisoner had been Cole Younger, but at the time they could prove nothing, and so had to let him go.

Now there were rewards posted everywhere. "Wanted: Frank James, alias McKinney; Dutch Charley Bayless, alias Randall, Borris, Davis, Bates, et cetera; Frank Toll; Sim Wan, thought to be Jessie James; George Parrotte, alias Big Nose George; Sandy Campbell, Tom Reed, Cully McDonald" and many more.

Laramie County's peace officer, T. Jeff Carr told Boz, "We have reason to believe this band is hiding out in the Medicine Bow country. But we can't seem to get them cornered. I've got a feeling, Boz, you're gonna be needed again."

Carr's prediction proved right. For in July, the weekly *Sentinel* newspaper came out bluntly and told the citizens: "For Sheriff—nothing to do with collecting taxes. We are interested in a man who will hunt down and bring to justice thieves and criminals that infest the country and in selecting N. K. Boswell for that responsibile position the Republican party has put forward the best man the country could furnish . . . Make this place an unpopular resort for criminals." But election day was several months away. And the road agents and outlaws now held the upper hand.

Aggressive and daring, the bandits moved down on the plains in August. They were holing up in the hills out of Medicine Bow, some eighty miles west of Laramie City. Here they concocted a plan to wreck a westbound train, carrying pay sacks destined for the Carbon coal miners.

They had it all plotted, and in the dusk of August 19, they struck, cutting the telegraph wire, loosening the spikes of the rails. They tied one end of the wire to the rail and dragged the other to their hideaway behind a huge embankment. In this spot, the jagged stone abutment of the road bed dipped some sixty feet. When they pulled the cable, they figured, it would dislocate the steel link and tumble the entire cargo.

The summer sun was setting behind the distant peaks, leaving the world streaked with a blood-red glow. Still, it was light enough for the bandits to see a man coming down the tracks toward them.

John Eric Brown, section foreman, had left his tool box on the Medicine Bow bridge and was returning to pick it up. Suddenly, as he walked, his sharp eyes spotted something unusual. He kept going, but his eyes never left the tracks. What he saw was the wire attached to the rail. Then he noticed the loose spikes scattered around on the ground.

"It was like walking on a keg of dynamite," he later related. "And I kept going until I reached my tools. I picked them up and retraced my steps as if I hadn't noticed the deadfall."

Brown heaved a sigh of relief when he was safely out of sight around the bend. But his alleviation was short lived. Down the tracks coming at frightful speed was the train, its headbeam lighting the roadbed.

Grabbing his lantern, Brown began frantically waving it. There was the sizzle of steam, the grind of brakes as the engine slowed. Brown motioned it to back up—return to the station, Como. There he came running, panting out what danger lay ahead. "And there were some hundred and fifty tourists on that train."

Everyone was up in arms when they heard of the daring scheme. The Union Pacific sent Superintendent Dickinson along with Sheriff Nottage to investigate. They found the hideaway and some loose stock left behind. The bandits had made a hurried getaway.

Since the attempted wreck was in Carbon County, its sheriff was summoned to track down the scoundrels. Two expert scouts, Robert Widdowfield of Carbon and Tip Vincent of Rawlins were deputized to sleuth the trail toward Elk Mountain.

"See if you can smoke the desperadoes out," was Sheriff Lowry's order.

One day went by. Two, then three. Sheriff Lowry became anxious. He organized a posse. Some five days later the bodies of Tip Vincent and Bob Widdowfield were found. They had been robbed of boots, guns, saddles and horses.

The murders of the two popular deputies aroused the populace as nothing previously had done. They were aware now of the dangerous and vicious characters on the prowl, and realized that no one was safe from them.

And so, as the first early autumnal frosts descended over the land, the border country faced a great crisis. With the Fetterman stages, their six-in-hand hitting for the north country, through a wilderness unpeopled except for occasional road ranches, with the pay money for the troopers coming in by train and being staged cross-country, with the English capital going up into the Powder River country to stock the ranges, and the bullion in the treasure boxes enroute to the railroad from the Black Hills mines, the pickings for the outlaws were fat. With the report of renewed holdups on the stage routes, it was now evident that the pack of outlaws had escaped out of the Elk Mountain country and were back on the trails.

Reports again came that Brown's Six Mile Station near Fort Fetterman had been held up. Stages, too, came in for renewed attacks, the masked bandits robbing men and pilfering the mail sacks and leaving the discarded contents strewn on the ground.

Deputies Robert Widdowfield and Tip Vincent were murdered near Carbon and their bodies hidden in the brush. *Carbon County Museum*

"The men who entered the Trabing Commissary are believed to be of the James Brothers' gang," the army reported to Washington, D.C.

These road agents," Marshal T. Jeff Carr wrote Boswell, "are leaving a trail of blood that would do justice to the whole Sioux nation. Gustave (Schnitzer) and I are hard put. I need more lawmen. And I intend to deputize some pronto."

Boswell was still a member of the Rocky Mountain Detectives, and it looked like Carr had in mind special assignments for him.

That November, Boz was elected sheriff with a big majority. There was a celebration that night—a bonfire at the post office intersection of Second and "A" Streets. The Laramie Silver Coronet band played and the citizens moved in and out of the crowd congratulating the winning candidates. They were clamoring for speeches. The lawyer Melville Brown and Senator Stephen Downey took the platform. Then someone called on Boz.

He was sitting beside Martha in the crowd, but he got up and took the stand. "I'm not much of a speaker," he told his cheering audience. "I'm more a man of action, I guess you'd say. You elected me to do a job. As your sheriff, I'll do the very best I can for you."

There was a great round of applause. Afterwards, there was a big supper and a dance at Ivinson Hall. It was past midnight when the elected sheriff and his wife returned to their little apartment. Boz sat at his desk drumming his fingers.

"I'm thinking of bringing me in a deputy, a man I have a powerful lot of faith in—Richard Butler, with his outstanding war record for bravery, could sure put the fear of the devil in these outlaws."

Butler was Martha's brother-in-law and the thought of her sister Annette coming to live in Laramie City was almost too good to be true!

Boz was to take office in January, but now in December, the citizens of the neighboring town, Rock Creek, couldn't wait. There was trouble brewing there. Bad trouble. They wired the United States marshal in Cheyenne, "Detail Boswell here at once."

116

Chapter 14

CAPTURING THE DEADWOOD
STAGE ROBBERS

Rock Creek, fifty miles west of Laramie City, was smack-dab in the grass-covered plains. It was flanked in the distance by the snow-capped Elk Mountain and the solitary sentinel Laramie Peak. Like two great eye teeth, these lofty summits sent lesser molars flanking toward the little cowtown.

Not only was Rock Creek a railhead, but it was also depot for the stage routes to Fetterman and Junction City, Montana.

Now this December day, 1878, C. D. Thayer, son of the ex-governor of the Territory, came in and cornered Boz. "The pay checks for the Fetterman soldiers are due in by rail, any day now. I have reason to believe a pack of cutthroats are hiding out in our hills. Perhaps scheming again some vicious crime. I'm going to notify the Union Pacific."

The people of the little community, too, were nervous and edgy. There were too many odd looking strangers drifting about. They sent a letter to the *Sentinel:* "We want action. We want these road agents captured."

After Thayer alerted the railroad officials in Omaha, they too were jumpy. They talked to Chief Dave Cook of the Rocky Mountain Detective Association. "Detail Boswell to the case at once."

The Chief knew Boz didn't take office until January, but this emergency couldn't wait. "You've scouted all that region before. You know it like a parson knows Scriptures. I'm commissioning you special detective and assigning you to do the job."

117

So Boz accepted. And the same day, Thayer again came in to report to the lawman latest developments.

"I got the word direct from one formerly of their band, Frank Howard. The gang sent him to my store to get supplies today. But Howard got weak-kneed and tipped me off."

"You mean the desperado, Frank Howard?"

"The same. But for some reason, he's conscience-stricken. He told me the whole plot. The gang is laying for the soldiers' pay car—plan to ditch the train it comes in on. Something has to be done, and fast. I've talked to Sheriff Nottage, but his attitude is why should he get himself shot up now that he's almost out of office. I've contacted the Union Pacific. It's offering $150 for the apprehension of each outlaw."

Hunting down the outlaws was a real challenge, and after all, Boz had told the voters he'd do the job. The opportunity was ripe. He was a United States marshal. Looked as though it might be now or never.

"I'll need a posse. And a special car from the Union Pacific."

In his quiet way, Boz went about making preparations. "We're up against a desperate ring that'll stop at nothing," he told Superintendent Dickinson. "I'd like to hand-pick from the volunteers. Experienced and brave men. You make arrangements with the company for a special car."

In the nearby hills of Rock Creek the stage robbers and railroad bandits hid out. *Wyoming State Historical Department*

In the darkness of Christmas Eve, when all Laramie City was enjoying the Yuletide festivities, Boz gathered his posse—ex-Sheriff Tom Dayton, J. T. Donahue, N. Thies, Tom Dougan, Ed Kerns, Brad Fonce, John Metcalk, J. F. Holcomb, Al LeRoy, Jack Fee, B. Halstead, F. Brown, and J. English.

"Aren't you going, Sheriff?" someone asked Nottage.

Only then, did the defeated Sheriff agree to accompany the party. The night was bitter cold when the expedition of grim and determined men outfitted with lethal weapons climbed aboard the special car.

"Sometime between candlelight and cock's crow," Boz said to Thayer, who was to meet them at Rock Creek. It was midnight when the train pulled into the little station.

"I've got the horses waiting," Thayer told the posse. "And I've got directions Howard gave me where they're camped."

It was then someone protested. "Surely we're not moving out tonight—trying to find them in the dark."

"Every minute is precious," Boz told his men. "We can't afford to waste it—if we're going to surprise the bandits, we must move at once."

Thayer handed Boz a sheet of paper. "The directions where the bandits are holed up," he said.

The posse was minus Sheriff Nottage, now. He'd been called back to Laramie City on urgent business.

It was about three o'clock Christmas morning when the men silently rode out on a lonely trail. The ground was covered with snow. A stiff wind was blowing and the mercury touched at thirty degrees below zero. A faint moon still showed in the sky when the men slipped up to the spot designated as the hideout. Cautiously, Boz scrutinized the terrain.

"They're not here," he told Dayton, "Only dead campfire ashes. They've moved on. But where?"

For a minute or two Boz stood. His busy mind like a pick-pocket, working its way through a crowd, was shifting and sorting ideas. Then he remembered a log cabin in the nearby vicinity where an old man lived.

"Ole Oleson runs a place over there called the Whisky Shop. I remember hearing someone say Ole also is employed by the Rock Creek Warehouse and has been friendly with the gang—in fact, he's suspected of furnishing food to them. Let's make a call on Ole."

Boz and his possemen pointed their horses toward the Whisky Shop in the gulch ahead. At the cabin, Boz stationed his men around it with three to guard the door. Then he knocked loudly.

"This is Boswell. Open the door, Ole."

It took a little time arousing the old man.

"Do you hear me?" Boz called again. "This is Boswell, United States marshal. Open the door, Ole."

Boz could hear a slight commotion—the falling of a chair, maybe.

"Who else is in there with you, Ole?"

"Only me. Only me," the voice inside spoke.

Boz pushed open the door. He could see a stand against the wall and Ole in his long woolen underwear was bending over it lighting a kerosene lamp. There were a couple of wolfskins on the floor near a buffalo hide covered cot. Boz saw a rifle over in the corner, and a gun belt with a forty-five over a chair back near the lamp stand. The old trader made a sudden move toward the revolver.

"No use reaching for that, Ole. I've got thirteen men just behind me who'll riddle you. We've come to take in the road agents and you to show us where they're holed up."

"I don't know a thing about what you're talkin'. Not a thing!"

At this point, Boz jabbed his rifle in the old fellow's ribs. "Mebbe this'll help your memory."

Boz suspicioned the old monger could be bribed, so he added, "And if you'll get some clothes on and take me and my men to their camp, I'll make it worth your while." In the lamplight, Boz began counting out greenbacks. He could see Ole pick up interest. "These'll be yours when you show us where the bandits are."

Sleepily, Ole began pulling on his pants. He'd accompany them to the road agents' new nesting place.

The posse mounted again, Ole and Boz leading the way. Silently, they rode in the frozen December night through a network of gulches and ravines. There was a faint moon in the sky when

120

Ole pointed ahead to a brush-shrouded camp under a protruding cliff. Then he turned to leave them.

"Just a minute," Boz spoke quietly. "How do we know you won't shoot at us or set off an alarm? You stay here. Fee, you take Ole prisoner. Hold him back in that thicket for the time being."

Boz dismounted then and motioned his men to tie their mounts in the willows. "Three of you scatter out. Cover different directions. The rest of us'll circle the camp."

Stealthily, their guns trained on the outlaws, muzzles like sore thumbs, Boz and his posse crept closer to the sleeping camp. Screened by naked thickets and snow bank abutments of the adjoining bluff, the desperadoes lay wrapped in blankets, their gun belts nearby on the ground. Around them, too, were saddles and overcoats. "They were accrued like pirates with loot from Treasure Island," Boz later told Cook.

The time was ripe to strike, and Boz motioned his men to circle the outlaw camp. They'd moved in now to take the bandits. But suddenly his hand went up, halting the possemen. Boz had crept to within fifteen yards of the sleeping men when, in the faint light from the moon, he had glimpsed a movement. A man was poking sticks into the embers of a fire and sliding a smoke-blackened coffee pot over the sputtering flame.

Now Boz gave the signal. The possemen cautiously crawled closer, their gun barrels aimed at the stubble-faced, snoring outlaws. Boz had his rifle sights set on the man at the fire. "Hands up! Hands up!"

The bandits came to with a start, sitting up suddenly and almost at once their hands shot into the air. All except one. The one kindling the fire. In the light Boz saw his sandy hair and pin-feathered beard and young face—nothing more than a kid.

But the youth was reaching for his pistol. In the same instant, sharp on the frost-bitten air, Boz, his voice curt, commanded, "You go for that gun and I'll kill you." As the youth hesitated, a shout came from one of the outlaws, "Kid," he yelled, "put that gun down. Can't you see he's got the drop on us!"

The youth paused, but seemed unconvinced. Again the leader shouted, "Put that gun down, you damned fool. Can't you see it's Boswell? He can spin a quarter with a shot at a hundred yards. And those others there behind him. Listen to me, and put that gun down or we'll all be dead. It's all up." The leader was behind the boy, grabbing his gun and dropping it immediately to the ground.

"Get your hands up," Boz ordered again, "all of you. Move in, men, and take them."

At this point, one of the volunteers came through the brush, herding another outlaw at the point of a rifle barrel. "Found him unhobbling the horses."

"Joe Manuse," Boz said. "I'd recognize him anywhere." Boz crowded Manuse and shoved him toward the circle of desperadoes. Manuse started to turn once, but the bore of Boz's gun pressed against his back.

"Manuse, don't put me to the trouble of cleaning my gun," Boz warned.

The outlaw felt the rifle barrel against his ribs and knew the lawman was serious.

"Now, all of you, round about and march with hands up. Let go of that knife, you there. Quick, before I trip this trigger."

The leader knew resistance was useless. "It's all up, boys," he told his gang. "Do as the marshal says."

The posse herded their sullen, disheveled prisoners into the railroad station at Rock Creek. There the Union Pacific had a car and engine waiting and the heroes of the day brought their captives into Laramie City. Boz and his men marched them down Second to "B" Street and on to the county jail where they were put under lock and key and the watchful eyes of several guards.

The word spread like wild fire: "Did you hear about our sheriff. He bagged the outlaws."

It was a strange way for Boz to celebrate Christmas Day. He came into the little apartment looking gaunt and tired. He saw the table set and he could smell the goose baking and the plum pudding steaming. Kissing Martha, then dropping into a chair, he took Minnie on his lap.

"Been on the go night and day. Mind if I help myself to a bite of something and hurry on?" Then rumpling the curls of his small blonde daughter, he said, "Santa's been kinda late this year. But he'll be along tonight. And you'll sing your song for me then."

122

Boz hurriedly ate a slice of goose, then he was on his way, heading for Ed Dickinson's office.

"We've got them," Boz told the railroad officials, "Harrington, Robie, Howard, Vassar, Manuse and Condon—the one they call the Kid. There are still others loose. Dutch Charley, Big Nose George, Cully Maxwell and John Irwin. But I have an idea Manuse knows a lot more than he lets on and could enlighten us on their whereabouts."

"I take it you mean to make Manuse talk."

"Right," Boz said, "And if you'll come with me, we'll take him out of the jail cell to a place I think may impress him with the consequences if he don't."

At the courthouse the jailor turned Manuse over to Boz and Dickinson. With the outlaw between them, they headed up South "B", making double time until they reached Seventh Street. Flanking their prisoner, they turned south. Here, between "C" and "D" Streets, and Seventh and Eighth, the Second Ward schoolhouse was going up. It was still in a rough state, but the walls were enclosed.

There were a number of raw rafter beams exposed. Boz backed his captive to the wall. With unshaved face, beady eyes and tight lips, Manuse stood sullenly slumped against it.

Boz began his probe: "What do you know about the Medicine Bow and Elk Mountain affair?"

The dark serpentine eyes of Manuse shifted, but he made no response.

"It will be better for your health if you answer my questions," Boz told the bandit. Still, Manuse remained sullen.

Boz took a meaningful coil of hemp from a sack he had been carrying. "Yes," he told the suddenly nervous Manuse, "You're about to be hoisted up." Boz called to Dickinson to help him tie the prisoner's arms. Then Boz began twisting the rope, knotting it.

"Ready to talk?"

Still Manuse pursed his lips tight and gave out no sign. The marshal tossed one end of the hemp up over the rafter, grabbing it as it came down, and securing it over the beam. He began pulling. Up went Manuse. Choking and sputtering and turning a deathly white, Manuse's eyes were bulging.

Boz slowly lowered the rope. But Manuse, his eyes snakelike, refused to talk. Once more the men adjusted the neckpiece and had Manuse dangling in the air again. They left him suspended, but suddenly Manuse, his face tinged blue, gasped, then stammered. "Enough. Enough. Please. I'll talk. I'll tell you what you want to know."

Back on the ground, it took the bandit several seconds to get his breath. Yes, he'd been with the gang. It was Dutch Charley's gang, but Dutch Charley had not been with them when they attempted the train wreck at Medicine Bow. He'd joined them later in Elk Mountain. In fact, it was Dutch Charley who'd fired the first shot on the deputies. "It happened this way," Manuse said:

"We were vacationing in the hills out of Medicine Bow between holdups when McKinney thought it a good idea to ditch the Union Pacific train. That August night we went into Medicine Bow and took what tools we needed from the railroad tool house. We stayed in hiding until the next evening along about dusk. We came down and loosened the fish plates from two rails. Then we hid behind the embankment to wait for the train."

"Did you see the section foreman?" Boz asked.

"Yes, we saw him. McKinney, our leader, wanted to kill him. But we talked him out of it. He was madder'n hell when the section foreman flagged that train down. Then we lit out for Rattlesnake Canyon."

The bandit paused, his snaky eyes looking at the ground. The two men waited patiently and when Manuse seemed hesitant, Boz prodded him with his gun barrel. "Go on," he ordered. "Tell us about rubbing out the deputies."

"Well, it was this way: The marshals was pushing us hard—hot on our trail. At the head of Rattlesnake Creek, they neared our camp site. We had a fire going and had to act fast, dousing the hot wood chunks into the streams. Then we hid in the brush where McKinney had cut a lookout.

"We saw Widdowfield come up on the campfire. He dismounted and stuck his hands in the ashes. We heard him say to the other officer, 'It's hot as hell. We're close on their heels.'

"That's when Dutch Charley and Big Nose George motioned us out and Dutch Charley said to the deputies, 'Yes, you sonsobitches, it's pretty damned hot all right and we're going to give

124

you a chance to find out how hot hell is.' He drew a bead on Widdowfield and fired. The deputy fell and the other sheriff, still in his saddle, saw he was outnumbered and gave spur to his horse. There was a dozen bullets flying at him. Big Nose and Dutch Charley and everybody shooting as fast as they could."

"And you all moved in and divided up the spoils, I take it," Boz said.

"Harrington took Widdowfield's saddle. Irwin got his guns. Big Nose put on his clothing. Dutch Charley's own horse was jaded and worn out so he shot him and mounted Widdowfield's roan. The other deputy's horse had bolted and left the country."

"Where's Dutch Charley and Big Nose and Irwin now?" Boz asked.

"Well, after the shooting, we got out of the country. Did some holdups on the stage road and up north. But we fell to quarreling amongst ourselves. There was trouble and Big Nose left us. Then McKinney and Sim Wan followed. With the blizzards on us, we decided to hole up in the Rock Creek gulch. We was about out of grub when Dutch Charley left. So we sent Frank Howard to Thayer's store to get supplies. John Irwin was to get some in Cheyenne. We figured there was less chance of him being recognized over there."

"How long ago did Irwin leave you?"

"Went about two days ago. He'll kill me fer informin' on him."

"The law'll protect you and you'll have a fair trial," Boz told the outlaw. "But before I take you back to the courthouse, I want a full description of what these men look like. Ed, you write down what he tells us."

"Well, Dutch Charley, he's a Prussian and big and blonde. And Big Nose, well you couldn't mistake him—his nose." In this way Boz and Ed Dickinson had a complete description of their wanted men. Then they returned Manuse to his jail cell. Boz left strict instructions with the guards to keep newspaper reporters from talking to the captives.

But there was no Chirstmas night at home for Boz after all. It would be up to Martha and Aunt Tye to take little Minnie over to Ingersoll's stable and show her what Santa had left. A fine pony and a miniature side saddle.

For Boz had boarded the train and was enroute to Cheyenne. Not a minute to waste as he slipped into McDaniels' Gold Room in the Capitol City. Walking with his easy stride, he made his way to the gaming table. Bearing himself with quiet dignity, he might have been mistaken for a minister if it had not been for the butts of his two revolvers bulging his coat at the hips.

Manuse had given him a complete description of Irwin. Besides, he had studied the outlaw's likeness on reward posters. Now the piercing eyes of Boz spotted his man. Irwin was shoving his chair from the gaming table, scooping up his winnings. So quietly did Boz take John Irwin prisoner that only the proprietor knew the arrest was made and that the notorious road agent Irwin was enroute with Boz to Laramie City.

Boz now had his covey of jailbirds lodged securely with guards taking shifts round the clock to make certain there were no breaks. Just when he thought he had everything under control, the presses began badgering him for details of the captures. Stubbornly, Boz remained silent. Much to his chagrin, the Laramie *Sentinel* announced the arrests but complained that an embargo had been put on the story. Dutch Charley and Big Nose George were still at large.

Chapter 15

THE HANGING OF DUTCH CHARLEY

Although he was not to be sworn in as sheriff of Albany County until the first week of the new year, Boswell was still a marshal on the force of the Rocky Mountain Detective Association, pledged to keep on the trail of the road agents. He must strike while that trail was hot.

Joe Manuse gave Boz minute descriptions of the outlaws and their destinations. Among the pack of badmen Manuse claimed were Frank and Jessie James, hiding under aliases, and diving in and out of the Big Horns and Montana's isolated haunts. Big Nose George Parrotte, too, had taken off for other environs, Manuse claiming his buddy had gone to the Cheyenne River country.

Dutch Charley, with all his aliases and string of accomplices, was the immediate concern of Boz. This desperado of Prussian lineage had kicked off the dust of his native Missouri and for over a year, had directed the various operations of his long riding riff-raff, men of deadly trades lured by the fat pickings of the cross-country stages and the railroad pay cars. These toughs had been drifting in and out of the frontier enjoying the profits of their free-booting and then roosting between holdups in the broad, hidden valley of Wyoming's hills.

Manuse, too, had tipped the lawman off to the whereabouts of Dutch Charley.

"He's trappin' on the Green."

It was the last week of December, 1878, when Boz told

127

Martha, "John LeFevre and I are leaving by train right away. Probably be gone for the New Year's."

Boz was buckling on his gun belt and taking his beaver coat from the wall peg. He hated missing Minnie's program at Mannchoir Hall, and the friendly get-togethers of the community.

And so New Year's Eve came to Laramie City once more. The falling snows shrouded the world in white and the wind whipped drifts up and down the streets. But even the below-zero weather could not halt the gaiety of the citizens.

The New York House was festive in holiday attire, its rows of spruce trees flanking the door. The Worth and the Frontier, too, decorated their walls and dining rooms with evergreens, and the midnight menus boasted fresh oysters and rare smoked salmon and Yorkshire puddings and fresh oranges. At Ivinson Hall was scheduled a ball of formal attire. Officers and their ladies from the nearby garrison would share the evening festivities. But for Martha, it was another holiday without her husband.

It was early morning of the New Year's third day that the town was awakened by an engine's shrill whistle. A little later, a hooded surrey came whisking from the depot into the intersection of Second and "A." In it two lawmen had a prisoner between them.

"Dutch Charley," voices were loud-keyed with tension. "They've caught Dutch Charley," and now it became a chorus amid a loud hurray!

Later, it was told how the two Albany county officers had tracked the fugitive into the isolated hills of the Green River country. Deputy LeFevre had come suddenly upon the bandit, and surprised him at his trap line, shackled him and brought him into the town of Green River. The two marshals then secreted him to await the next eastbound train. So swiftly and stealthily did the officers act, that only the railroad crew was aware that the dangerous road agent was barricaded in the baggage car, headed for Laramie City.

But you couldn't keep a catch like Dutch Charley secret. Editor Hayford was bound to scoop the story: "Taken in," he reported to his readers, "another of the Vincent-Widdowfield murderers was captured this week in Green River by John LeFevre. He gives his name as Bayless and sometimes Davis. He is known as Dutch Charley and was one of the worst of the gang. Positive evidence is in the hands of the authorities that he was involved in the Elk Mountain murders."

Boz had a bunch of real badmen locked up—over eighty prisoners crowded into thirty-nine cells.

"It's going to take a powerful lot of watching," he told the county commissioners. So the board immediately appointed Ed Kern and Richard Butler to the force.

A couple of days later, Boz received word that one of the road agents, John Vassar, who was still at large, had shown up in Leadville, Colorado.

"I'll be away no longer than I can help," he told his deputies, "But if Carbon County asks for Dutch Charley, be sure you move him in secret. The people are all stirred up, and that sin-steeped old rouge won't have a chance if they lay hands on him."

Boz was barely on his way to Leadville when Carbon County requested Dutch Charley be brought to Rawlins. Kerns was assigned to accompany the prisoner.

It was a cold, blustery Sunday night, January 5th, when the deputy whisked Dutch Charley into an express car on Number Three. Stacking trunks to form a high wall, he secreted his handcuffed man within the enclosure.

The railroad company had agreed that the train would barely pause in Carbon, home of the murdered Widdowfield. It would take on fuel and proceed immediately westward. Besides, it was Sunday, and the citizens would not be out on the streets, so reasoned the authorities.

But someone had tipped off the Carbonites. Was it Frank Howard, who was now riding detective for the Union Pacific? Or was it a Laramie friend of Bob Widdowfield? Or perhaps someone in Rawlins?

At any rate, when the engine pulled up to the docks, an army of determined and intent masked men boarded the train. Grimly efficient, they unburdened the train crew of its immediate duties, holding engineer, conductor and brakeman at gun point. Then a number of men climbed into the baggage car. Pushing over the barricade, they relieved Kerns of his guns. They took Dutch Charley into custody.

"Please men," begged the murderer as he felt the revolver

butts punching his ribs, "Give me a sporting chance." Then he saw a coil of rope. " Please, I beg of you, don't string me up. Shoot me, but don't string me up!"

The enraged citizens only mocked him. They shuffled him off the train into the shadows of the schoolhouse where he confessed his fiendish crime. They paraded him down Main Street to a telegraph pole. "This," they told him, "is a dying place for outlaws."

Dutch Charley cowered again. Two men were fastening a noose around his neck. "Get up on that keg," they ordered.

It was then Dutch Charley started to say something, "Joe Manuse, he . . ."

That was when Frank Howard, one of his former pals in crime, but now turned state's evidence and detective for the Union Pacific, kicked the barrel from under Dutch Charley.

The limp body of the bandit swung all night from the crossbeam. The sun was up and gliding down again behind Elk Mountain when the county coroner came from Rawlins. He ordered the corpse cut down and pronounced Dutch Charley Bayless, Randall, Davis, Boris, et cetera, dead from exposure.

The docket of the Albany County district court that early spring of 1879 read like a wild west roster. Corraled and awaiting

The coal mining town of Carbon, Wyoming, 1875, where angry citizens took Dutch Charley from train and hanged him. *Union Pacific collection*

130

trial was a bevy of desperadoes. Some for grand larceny, some for murder, some for mayhem, some for horse stealing, some for knowingly killing neat cattle, and two for sodomy.

One by one, the outlaws were called for trial. Albany County, Territory of Wyoming: Robbery, John Irwin. This road agent admitted to participating in the holdup of the Deadwood Stage the previous September in which his pal Frank Towle was killed, also that he had been in on the Widdowfield-Vincent murders.

The Kid, too, admitted his guilt. Both were sentenced to life in the penitentiary across the Laramie River.

Trials for such gross offenses took days. It was no child's play guarding these desperadoes. The security of the wooden cells was totally inadequate, but it took a break and a near escape of one outlaw to convince the commissioners something must be done at once.

One of the bandits had taken up a flagstone in the bottom of his cell, dug three feet down under the inside wall, then tunneled up sixteen feet outside to the surface. He had the hole big enough to squirm his way to the early morning sunlight.

But when he lifted his eyes joyously to anticipated freedom, he was looking into the barrel of Butler's and Boswell's guns. The would-be fugitive lost no time accepting their invitation to worm himself back inside.

"No telling what they may try next," the sheriff told his deputy.

So again Boz went before the county commissioners— James McGibbon, G. B. Grow and John Meldrum. "I think it would be well worth the expense of removing the old jail cells in the undercroft and replacing them with steel ones." The board agreed and it also added more guards.

One by one, the men were tried. John Vassar and Fred Robie were sentenced to seven years in the penitentiary. Joe Manuse admitted he was wearing Boone May's overcoat—that he'd taken it in the stage stick-up of September 13th. He also confessed to participating in other robberies and that he was a member of the gang attempting the Medicine Bow train wreck. Again the Carbon County officials stepped in to ask that Manuse be turned over to them.

Transporting the outlaw to Rawlins had its dangers. The desperado fought removal. He was certain his fate would be the same as that of Dutch Charley.

"You'll have the protection of the law," Boz told him. "I'll personally see to that."

So plans began in secret on an April day in 1879 to convey Manuse over the same route taken by his confederate in crime on the previous January night. Boz secured co-operation from the Union Pacific officials as well as having a second escort, Under-Sheriff Jim Rankin of Carbon County.

It was a long journey, crossing bridges and ravines and sagebrush tablelands. Not until later did the lawmen know that with them on that trip rode two journalists, Charles Bramel and L. Pease. These editors were certain that a hanging was in the offing and they were determined to have a first-hand account. At Medicine Bow they slipped from their hiding place to ride the cowcatcher into Carbon.

As the train neared the coal town, Boz quietly moved through the passenger car, asking the ladies if they would mind retiring to the pullman where they'd be more comfortable. Next he requested of the brakeman, "Pull down the window shades of all the passenger cars, and lock the doors."

Boz and Rankin now had their prisoner alone in one car, handcuffed. Rankin took a stand at one exit. Boz, his prisoner seated nearby, stood at the opposite one. He could not help noticing the white-faced and trembling Manuse.

"If anyone boards this train," he told his prisoner, "I'll give you two six-shooters. You are entitled to defend yourself."

But Rankin had pulled a bit of strategy before leaving his county seat. He'd summoned a grand jury to convene there, and he'd called a number of the leading citizens of Carbon to appear on it. When the engine of Number Three pulled into the station, that town was as dead as a cemetery.

A great sigh of relief came from Manuse when the engine hit the frog rail and rounded the curve heading up Simpson Hill. The two newsmen had abandoned their precarious seats outside and now were admitted to the passenger car.

"Damn it," said Pease. "To think I made this trip for nothing. I'd planned on seeing a real old-fashioned lynching."

132

The outlaw chase kept Boswell busy all during the spring and early summer of '79. It was Al Douglas next. For sometime the Rock Creek-Fetterman Stage officials had been certain this man had been blackmailing their line, and tipping off the highway robbers. One day the superintendent brought the sheriff a note he'd retrieved from Douglas signed "Henry Ward Beecher."

It was this same signature officers had found near the campfire ashes at the Vincent-Widdowfield murder scene. Al Douglas had been employed for a time as manager of the Rock Creek-Fetterman Stage line. Boz had always been a little suspicious of him. Now, turning to the stage representative, he said simply, "Come on. Let's go after him."

It was May 18, 1879 when they captured Douglas. At the trial Douglas admitted signing his tip-offs to the robbers, but the authorities had no proof he'd actually participated in the holdups. Judge Blake sentenced him to one year in the penitentiary. And the court gave the same sentence to the next prisoners appearing before him—Myron Blair, alias Buffalo Sam, convicted of grand larceny, John Little and William Nash, both for robbery.

When Boz marched the convicts across the river, assigning them to Warden Ned Spicer, he also had with him Charles Condon, alias The Kid, surly and troublesome.

"How long for him?" asked Spicer.

"Life," Boz told him.

"Like hell," The Kid spouted out, "There's no fence high enough to hold me."

And he was right. The summer had barely dawned when word spread like grassfire that The Kid had escaped.

"Two of my guards took departing shots at him, but he was lightning-fast," Spicer told Boz. "The Kid just out-distanced everybody's bullets."

The alert was sounded for every available lawman to get on the trail, scour all the marshes and adjoining land.

"He couldn't have got too far away," Spicer reasoned.

Boswell tracked The Kid to Mike Carroll's homestead. There, in the kitchen, sat the young fugitive, nonchalantly devouring pieces of Mrs. Carroll's luscious custard pie.

"But he's just a boy," Mrs. Carroll told the sheriff.

"Boy or not," Boz told her, "he's trigger happy and sure no

fit playmate for your Lizzie or Tessie. And so I'll have to ask you to excuse him."

So, once more The Kid was escorted back to be locked up with the other criminals in the "Big House" across the Laramie River.

Chapter 16

A PLEASURE—
BRINGING IN BIG NOSE GEORGE

The sands of 1879 sifted on. By late August N. K. was in the saddle again, hunting down another road agent. This one (going by the name of Hines) had been giving the officers a bad time. He'd been diving in and out of ranchers' line camps robbing them of all available food and bedding. Boz decided to go it alone after this desperado because he could make tracks faster that way. Packing into the ravines of Papoose Canyon, he traveled a dim trail amid much timbered terrain.

A day later Boz picked up Hines. No one seemed to know the details for Boz modestly told his friends, "I surprised him and took him without too much trouble. He was so flabbergasted, I guess, that anyone would catch up with him in that wild country that he handed over his gun without too much resistance."

What Boz did not relate at that time was how he forced Hines to mount his stolen horse, then with the prisoner's hands securely cuffed to the saddle horn, the bandit was deposited some twenty-four hours later in the county bailiwick.

Hardly had this mission been accomplished when Sheriff Boswell was notified by Denver authorities that a couple of thieves wanted in Albany County had been spotted in the Colorado city. He brought the culprits back and the editor of the *Sentinel* praised the lawman's prowess: "Boz makes the boss sheriff. He went down to Denver this week and bagged a brace of horse thieves."

But there was still Cully Maxwell and Big Nose George at large. He wouldn't rest until those two had been accounted for. But the hunt was interrupted by a more immediate cause for alarm. All hell had broken loose on the Ute Indian reservation where the agent, Nathan Meeker, was dictating their way of life. The agent's first upsetting act was to move their reserve fifteen miles below the old location on White River. They were furious.

"I shall also cut every Indian down to the starvation point if he will not work," was Meeker's threat. This, N. K. knew, was asking for sure trouble.

True, the Ute reservation was in Colorado, but old Chief Ouray's braves hunted in the hills of the North Park, bordering Wyoming Territory. Here were many mines and scattered ranches. Boz feared that any tyrannical treatment by Meeker would send the redmen into the North Park country. Although Ouray was friendly, yet Colorow was apt to go on the war path anytime.

Boz guessed right. The Utes, so incensed over Meeker's despotic treatment, rebelled. Ouray was away hunting deer, so one of them, a half-breed named Johnson, thrashed Meeker and chased him out of his agency house.

The battle was on. The agent requested troops be sent in at once. The gallant Major Thomas Thornburgh rode out with his companies of cavalry and infantry from Fort Fred Steele on the Platte. He ran head on with Colorow's warriors.

Boz, hearing of the battle of Red Canyon on the Milk River in which Major Thornburgh was ambushed and killed, knew that the settlers at North Park were now in danger. Whenever bullets and arrows were let loose against each other, it set warriors into a frenzy. He figured the hills would be alive with redmen.

"There's hardly a soldier left at Fort Sanders," Boz told his commissioners. "The companies have been moved out to the assistance of Thornburgh. But the Fourth Infantry Band is still there and the garrison could afford protection for the North Park settlers."

"Take your volunteers," Meldrum told him, "and alert these people."

At the head of the group riding into the North Park country, was Mortimer Grant, cousin of the famous general. Both Boz and

136

Grant owned mines up there at what was the Cinnabar City settlement. Both men knew the country. "We were a bunch of Paul Reveres," N. K. later said, "riding like hell to warn the people that the Utes were coming. That they'd better load up their wagons and get down inside Fort Sanders' stockade."

But Boz, himself, didn't get out in time to avoid a skirmish.

"While we were at the mines," he later told his cronies, "an old-timer named Frank Crout rode in, yelling to us that Utes were on the rampage and off the reservation. Everyone caught his horse and was ready to leave when I looked to the hills about two miles above the mine. I saw the Indians riding toward us. I had a wild unbroke colt and he bolted out from under me."

In this way, Boz was left behind the others, the redmen cutting him off. He made a run for a dugout which had a log lean-to. The space behind it was like a cellar, spaded out into the hillslope. There was a three-foot opening boarded with slats. Boz squeezed through it.

As he lay in hiding, he could hear the warriors going through the lean-to whacking and destroying everything in sight. Then he heard them leave, slamming the door behind.

From outside came the sounds of the Indians whooping and hollering. The cattle were bawling, too, and that meant the Utes were raiding the herd. Looking through a crack in the logs, he saw them dragging a couple of cows. These they butchered and then built a fire in the corral. As the meat roasted over the flames, the warriors licked the juices from their fingers.

Boz crawled back into the dugout and lay there all day. At dusk, the Indians returned to the shanty and with a flaming stick, set it afire. Now the logs of the wall began crumbling all around him. But the loose dirt fell into some of the flames and kept it from spreading to the roof. "The smoke became unbearable. I decided they might as well scalp me as to suffocate me." So when darkness descended and the wind died down and the Indians had crawled off in the grass, Boz slipped out of his hideout and crept slowly toward the direction of the meadows. Luckily, a horse was still there. "I knew I could hide my tracks along the creek bed if I could make it there. So I led the horse and headed for Douglas Creek. Though almost frozen to death, I followed it all night. At daybreak, I hid in the brush of the mountains."

137

A little later he hit out again. He came upon the body of an old-timer, Jim Sparks. He'd been scalped and left on the trail.

Finally, he caught up with some soldiers from Fort Sanders, and joined them scouting the area. At the Keystone Mine they found a nine-year-old boy who'd been lost from his family. By now, everyone was practically starved, so Boz said, "Let's stop and kill a venison and spend the night in this cabin."

The next day they headed back toward civilization. On the way they met some soldiers and the boy's father. And all thanked their lucky stars they were still alive.

For a brief time that autumn, the Ute Indian trouble took his mind off rounding up the last of the road agents. And there was a day when he was designated a member of the honor guard to escort General Grant passing through Laramie by train to Cheyenne. With him on this assignment went Mortimer Grant, John Donnellan and Bill Holliday.

New Year's Day, 1880, dawned bright and sunny in Laramie City. The town was celebrating Leap Year and because the census report still admitted to a woman shortage on the frontier, the eligible bachelors were taking it on themselves to hold open house and receive calls from the town's gentle tamers.

The newspaper boasted that Laramie City outdid Denver by the number of births that year—234 to 231. And the stockyards shipped 11,000 head of cattle. The town, too, the *Sentinel* said, was becoming citified—that George Vaughn was lettering the names of the streets, and numbering the houses.

So the sheriff was counting his days in office and anxious to round up the remaining renegades at large, so he could settle down on his productive ranch on the Big Laramie.

It was April, 1880, when Boz received word that Cully Maxwell had been captured. He had committed a number of thefts along the Blackhills' Road and was now reposing in the hoosegow at Yankton, Dakota Territory. Sheriff Boswell immediately requisitioned that the road agent be returned to Albany County to stand trial.

But Cully had no hankering to be subjected to the possible treatment Wyoming had given his sidekick, Dutch Charley. He fought by means of writ and appeals to stay in Yankton. Despite his persistent efforts, the law decreed that he be returned to the scene of his more heinous crime, and Albany County's sheriff was commissioned to bring him back.

Boz was preparing for this trip when he received notice from the Dakota sheriff that Cully Maxwell had escaped. The outlaw had sawed a bar from the window using a steel shank which he had concealed in the sole of his boot.

But the bandit's whereabouts was to remain a mystery for only a short time. The Union Pacific and the Dakota authorities offered a $2200 reward for his capture. The "Wanted" posters did the job.

And right on the heels of this in July, 1880, came word from Miles City, Montana, that officials had Big Nose George in custody. The outlaw, likkered to the gills, had run head on with Tom Irvine, Sheriff, and X. Biedler, United States marshal, on Miles City's main street.

"Big Nose" George Parrotte, road agent and bandit. *Union Pacific collection*

Wyoming was notified to come get its man. Rankin from Carbon County was assigned this job. It was a trip of several hundred miles by way of Yankton and Omaha. It would require several transfers. Rankin called on Boswell, "I need help getting my man back into Wyoming." Albany County's sheriff replied, "It will be my pleasure."

So the two lawmen, with their prisoner securely shackled and barricaded in the express car, began the journey back to Wyoming. Enroute, they discussed the method of getting him to the Carbon County jail.

Said Rankin, "We've got to make sure the days of Big Nose's twiddling his gunman thumb at the law is over. Can't take a chance on his escape." So the lawmen decided to deposit Big Nose first in the Laramie jail, and then a few nights later, they'd remove him to Rawlins.

It was a dark night in August when the two sheriffs circled the outskirts of Laramie City with their prisoner. They crossed the tracks and at the west end of town, the train pulled to a stop. They loaded Parrotte from the opposite side of the depot, two miles out. Rankin would continue with his prisoner to Rawlins.

"How the Carbonites got wind of it, I'll never know," Rankin said later. "Hell, when we pulled up to the depot, they were there to meet us. If I hadn't been outnumbered, I'd have plugged the leaders—leading citizens or not. As it was, I didn't have a chance. They overpowered me and took Parrotte down the street. They wanted a full confession. They had him dangling until he was blue in the face. He told them, 'My name is George Francis Warden.' And he told us McKinney was really Frank James. That Sim Wan was Jessie. But that both had kicked off Wyoming's dust for Kansas."

The Carbonites elevated Big Nose the fourth time in order to get more details. They were at last satisified—his story substantiated the information on the gang as given Boz by Manuse that Christmas Day almost two years ago.

They would turn Big Nose over on condition the law gave him his just deservings. At last Rankin had his prisoner shackled and lodged behind bars in the jail of his own county seat.

But keeping the capture of Big Nose secret was impossible. The reporters came swarming and all sorts of stories circulated.

Men, fearful that the bandit would make a break, stood on street corners and chafed and cursed.

Since Boswell was a principal in bringing the outlaw back to the scene of his fiendish crime and since he was called as a witness in the trial, it is well to report here the case of the Territory of Wyoming, County of Carbon, versus George Parrotte:

Members of the searching party who found the remains of Deputies Vincent and Widdowfield that summer day two years ago were subpoenaed. Among these were Jim Rankin, Jesse Wallace, William Ike, George Swansson, John Foote, Bill Daley.

The courtroom was filled the day Big Nose was arraigned. He was called to take the stand and suddenly he surprised Judge Jacob Howe, by his statement' "Your Honor, I would like to change my plea of guilty. My confession was made under duress." The court granted his request and set a subsequent day for trial, remanding Parrotte to jail "to think the matter over."

It was the end of the month before the trial was resumed. Big Nose again requested the indulgence of the Court, stating his plea he "would like to change to guilty."

The snows were falling and early winter was settling over the land when the case was resumed. The posse's testimony related the discovery of the deputies' bodies in Rattlesnake Canyon, near Elk Mountain.

"The men had been dead about a week." Rankin related. "The remains were bloated and swollen in the August sun. Sticks had been thrown over them."

"We found old boots thrown away, old saddle girths and old stirrups discarded," was Bill Daley's testimony.

Big Nose admitted his part in the murders, telling of the plot to ditch the train, its failure and their flight to Elk Mountain. "We were waiting to rest up. We put a guard out. Then we saw the two men riding on our trail. I heard the tallest man say 'We must be very close to them.' Then Frank Towle fired and the man fell in the hot ashes. The balance of us fired at the other man. Some of our men went out to rob them of boots, guns and coats. Dutch Charley took one of them's Sharps rifle and throwed away his own carbine. We dragged the dead men into the brush. Yes, I guess we fired about twenty shots to kill him. I done just about as

141

much shooting as any of the balance of them and I am just as guilty as they are. Yes, I been in the country several years."

Concerning the gang's next move Big Nose admitted, "There was bad blood between us. Frank Towle left first and I heard he'd been killed in the Black Hills Stage Line holdup. Some of us went up into the north in Goose Creek country. Then we had some more troubles and some of us left for the Cheyenne River and some went down to the railroad again. I heard Dutch Charley went to Fort Benton and then back to the Wyoming country."

Parrotte was found guilty of murder in the first degree and remanded for sentence. On a gloomy day with skies overcast, December 15, 1880, Judge William Peck summoned the governor of the Territory, the county and city officers and members of the clergy to be present at court while he pronounced: "I do hereby sentence George Parrotte to be hung on April 2, 1881, between the hours of ten and four o'clock at the place within the County of Carbon, Territory of Wyoming, provided for that purpose, and the Court orders the transcript of the testimony be made and filed in the court journal."

But the outlaw, now confined to his cell to await execution, began maneuvering for delay. He went on a hunger strike, and then feigned conversion to religion, quoting Bible passages and humming church hymns.

In Laramie City, Boz, hearing that the bandit's attorneys were considering a plea of insanity for their client, fretted to his deputy, "I'll sure sleep a lot sounder when I know Big Nose's outlaw career is over."

142

Chapter 17

BIG NOSE MAKES A BREAK

Election day, November, 1880, rolled around, and again Boz had a challenger on the ballot. This time J. T. Holliday sought the voters' approval. But men gathering on the street corners or gabbing in saloons agreed that their sheriff had done himself proud.

"No use letting a new crop of criminals get any ideas," they said.

"And the ladies turned out well," reported the *Sentinel* editor, "the voting was quiet, peaceful and in good order. Here, there was none of the drunken sprees characteristic of so many of our Western Sister states."

So January, 1881, Boz was again sworn in as Albany County sheriff. Two months went by and the trial in Carbon County for Big Nose George Parrotte was set. Since Boswell was involved in bringing the desperado back, he was subpoenaed. It is well here to repeat the story of the outlaw's attempted escape. It happened this way:

It was the supper hour that Tuesday, and the jail was unusually quiet—like the lull before the hurricane. The sheriff was out of town, but his jailor, Bob Rankin (brother of Deputy Jim Rankin) was the custodian of Big Nose. That evening, he went to the bullpen carrying the prisoner's supper tray.

When Rankin entered, the outlaw was ready for him. Sometime during the afternoon, he had managed to sharpen a table knife and saw a bolt off a link of his shackles. He then hid in the water closet awaiting his opportunity. Using the shackles as his weapon, he slugged the jailor with a vicious blow to the head. The supper tray went clattering and Big Nose struck a second blow.

Rankin, stunned badly, staggered backward just as the outlaw raised the weapon for a third blow. Unexpectedly, the jailor rallied, sidestepped, and like a cougar, his fist doubled, landed a telling punch to the head of the desperado. The dazed badman hit hard against the wall and went down. Rankin rushed for the outside of the bullpen, yelling as he went, "My gun. My gun. Bring my gun."

The commotion and the shouts brought his wife on the run. With a pistol, she rushed toward the jail, firing it into the air as she ran. When she arrived on the scene, her husband, wavering on unconsciousness, lay sprawled in a pool of blood.

Seeing the open grated door, Mrs. Rankin rushed to it, pulled it shut and locked it. In the meantime, Big Nose still in a daze from the jailor's blow, had made for the sanctum of the water closet.

But, by this time, the report of the pistol fired by the jailor's wife had brought a number of people from outside into the jail. In short order, they had Parrotte in chains again and securely locked inside his cell.

From the courthouse word spread quickly: "Big Nose has attempted a break!"

"Jailor Rankin is badly injured, slugged by Big Nose."

Now everywhere on the street corners little knots of men gathered and began whispering.

It was about ten o'clock when the conversations died down and the crowds seemed to have disappeared. But a few minutes later, men in twos were noticed going to the courthouse.

About eleven o'clock, Rankin was resting in his quarters when Simms, the guard, heard a knock on the door. He heard voices, too, loud—keyed with tension.

"I can't admit you. It's too late. The rules are against visitors at this late hour," the guard told them.

There was a buzzing of male voices and a great clamor. Suddenly, the door was burst off its hinges and an army of grim masked men with guns plainly visible, pushed into the room.

144

Covering the guard with their sixguns and rifles, the men swarmed forward. It was all done so quickly that Simms could only throw up his hands as they shoved him into a back seat.

The silent but determined men moved into Jailor Rankin's room where they found him bandaged and on a couch. Gently, but firmly, they took the key from his pocket and left.

Inside the jail, the posse had difficulty opening Big Nose's cell door and so they battered it down with an axe. At last they had the cowering white-faced outlaw in custody. They dragged him from the jail, out into the night air and across the courtyard.

At the edge of the grounds, they encountered Special Guard John London who was coming on duty.

"It'll be best for your health," they told him, "if you just take a walk."

As this advice was backed up by revolvers and rifles, the guard was easily persuaded to accept their counsel.

It was now evident that there was to be a hanging. At least a hundred of the morbidly curious gathered on the street to watch the bandit cash in his chips. The men in charge all wore masks. They had a coil of hemp around a telephone pole, and someone brought a barrel and deposited Big Nose on it. Another man, white masked, fastened the other end of the rope around the outlaw's neck. Big Nose looked gray and sick as he heard someone give the order to kick the barrel.

But the rope was too long and the desperado fell to the ground. As they were adjusting the rope, Big Nose, ashen and trembling, begged, "It's a shame to take a man's life this way. Give me time and I will climb the ladder myself, and when I get high enough, I'll jump off. Or for God's sake, someone shoot me. Don't let me choke to death!"

But the resolute men soon had George dangling in mid-air, his arms limp at his sides. A little later a coroner came and pronounced Big Nose George launched into eternity. His body was cut down and taken to Bill Daley's funeral parlor where an inquest was held. The verdict rendered was 'Big Nose George Parrotte was hanged by his neck with a rope until dead.'

Immediately, a young medico who'd witnessed the hanging asked for the remains of Big Nose. "For scientific purposes—the brains and skull of an outlaw ought to make interesting study!"

145

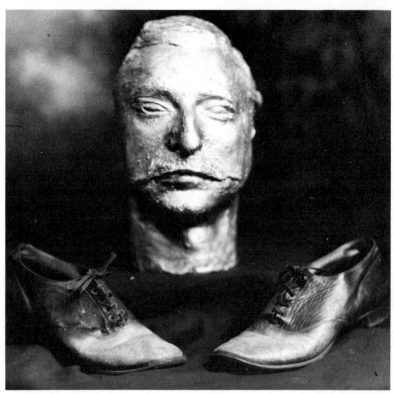

Death Mask and shoes made from the skin of Big Nose George.

Boz was to know this practitioner as John Osborne, later governor of Wyoming. But that night, the doctor was intent on obtaining the grey matter inside the cranium of the dead bandit for examination. He took the body, too. The skin was so tough, he decided to have it tanned. He had a pair of two-tone dress shoes fashioned from the hide off the thighs. A medicine bag he had made from the skin of Parrotte's chest. Boz later viewed these items in Rawlins when he visited the bank where Osborne, a director once, had them displayed.

The top of Parrotte's skull was severed and presented to Osborne's pretty red-haired assistant, Dr. Lillian Heath, who in turn gave it to the Union Pacific Museum in Omaha to exhibit.

After all the dissecting, the badmen's bones were tossed into a whisky barrel and buried right on Cedar Street, a main thoroughfare of the town. The grave, unmarked, for a time was visited by a number of curiosity seekers and school children.

The bones of "Big Nose" George Parrotte, long forgotten, were dug up in downtown Rawlins, Wyoming, May 11, 1950, when workmen were excavating for the erection of a modern store building.   *Union Pacific collection*

"Someday they'll be digging up that skeleton and wondering whose and why," Albany County's lawman predicted.

For Boz had seen lone graves before. Right here in Laramie City where they were excavating for newer and more modern buildings, human bones were occasionally dug up. And there were enough of those first-year citizens around to recall the morgue of the hoodlum Bosses Five who'd ruled the town and dumped corpses with such careless abandon under their shacks of ill-fame. And just past Fourth Street adjoining the Baptist Church, a builder had unearthed a grave.

"That," Boz told the editor of the new *Boomerang* publication, "was where Laramie City had its first burial ground. Forty-two graves. Sheriff Dayton had his prisoners do that chore back in '73. Removed them to the new cemetery farther out. Must have overlooked this one."

Well, 1881 was moving right along. The brigand band of road agents was at last broken. Boz heard that the James Brothers had drifted out of the Territory and he knew the Daltons had sold their house on Seventh. Still, he was determined that none of the embers of the lawlessness should flare into another holocaust to threaten the peace and settlement of this land. And he kept in constant touch with James Stirling, town constable—the two working hand in hand to suppress the lawless.

"About the Red Light District," Stirling confided to Boz, "what do you think about closing the houses up? Some of the lads out at the Fort tell me the girls are rosier and rounder and more graceful dancers than the town girls. There are them out there that say 'the sporting gals can make us feel that we don't give a damn if its war or peace.' "

"If I were you," Boz told the constable, "I'd hang padlocks on the buildings and run them out of town. They're trouble-makers. They can be the beginnings of a lot of lawlessness—plying the young Blue Coats with their brazen wiles."

"But," the town marshal confided, "half of them houses are owned by some of the town's leading citizens. They don't care about that part being known so they send their clerks to collect the rents. I don't think they'll like me closing them down."

"To hell with those kind of citizens," Boz said, "I talked with

148

County Attorney Blake this morning. He'll back us up and get the convictions."

So, one by one, the bawdy houses were shut down, and the protesting Madams chased out of town. There was Dolly and Kate and Lulu and Nellie and Alice and Belle and Marie all arrested, fined and shipped out of town.

All in all, Laramie City showed evidence of settling down. There were signs of growing prosperity and culture, too. Professor William Marquardt and his wife Lulu, talented musicians, had taken up residence and organized the Mannerchoir Society. They were giving voice, violin and piano lessons. Minnie Boswell was one of their outstanding pupils. Gus and Charley Trabing had closed their holdings in the north country and were back in town. They opened a big warehouse fronting on two streets, so they could carry on a territorial mail order business. And Charley Kuster was erecting a fine stone structure on Front and "A" Streets. Henry and Katherine Bath were enlarging their hotel—of stone, too. W. J. Holliday announced plans for the construction of a new opera house "to be the largest one west of the Missouri River."

The telephone to connect Laramie with Cheyenne was completed. And the town boasted a telephone exchange. The *Laramie Boomerang*, Bill Nye's new publication, had invested in the latest invention—a power press.

The older newspaper, *The Sentinel*, poked fun of its competitor. Editor Hayford told his readers: "Eli Perkins gets $100 for making an ass out of himself while Editor Nye—well, it was always so—people will pay more for the imitation than the genuine article."

Nye had selected a donkey for his newspaper coat of arms, and the competing editor explained to his reading public that "a particularly peculiar trait of the jackass when helped out of the mire will turn and kick his benefactors as soon as his feet touch solid ground."

The winter of '81 and '82 was a long and harsh one, beleaguered by blizzards. The snows and below-zero weather seemed to know no let up. All during March and April, they caused the train crews trouble. The drifts piled to fifteen feet depths and snow and ice covered the tracks. The old snowsheds, built in the '70's along

149

the line, were a God-send. Trainmen told Boz, "It's like railroading in a barn, but they let us get through in spite of the storms."

It was April that year Boz received notice that Jessie James was dead. He recalled how once he'd had Jessie locked up right in the town klink, but the bandit had not been one of the feathers in the lawman's cap. Jessie had been shot and killed by Robert Ford in St. Joseph, Missouri. Another badman accounted for!

More and more, Boz was looking forward to his termination as a law enforcer. He had a big ranch on the river, and a cozy bungalow in Laramie City. Not that his ambitions soared to the heights of some of his rich rancher friends—Ora Haley, the Swans, Oerlichs, Teschmacher, Fred Hess, Warren, John Clay or the Careys. They were giants stalking this land, regarded by others as "brilliant successes intent on keeping their big spreads unfenced as their own."

Already Swan had finished a test case on the Homesteaders' Rights—the fence case it was called. "Territory of Wyoming versus Alexander Swan." And Alex had lost. Now he, along with a lot of the other big stockmen, were screaming to High Heavens that the homesteaders had them in the "Hug of Death." The beginning of another great shadow settling over this land, although Boz did not know it then.

It was this year, too, that the Honorable James Blaine of Maine procured a pardon for Charles Condon, The Kid, whom Boz had captured in the Rock Creek vicinity along with those other road agents Christmas Day of '78.

"Charley comes from a good family," Blaine told the sheriff. "His parents are my good friends. They want him back home with them in Maine."

"I'm always glad to see a young man given another chance," N. K. told the Senator. "I'm certain he was an adventurous youngster fallen into bad company. He's done time enough in prison now to know it's not the best way to spend a lifetime!"

Early that summer, Boz told the voters he'd not be a candidate for sheriff in the November election. But he accepted the honor of being a delegate to the Territorial Convention which would be held in Green River.

In August, General Phil Sheridan, with his party of dignitaries arrived in Laramie enroute to view the wonders of Yellowstone Park. Albany County's sheriff was assigned as official escort to the famed general. Before they left, the honored guest expressed a desire to visit the now abandoned Fort Sanders where he'd once served.

A highlight of September was the tour of Her Highness Princess Louise and her royal party from Europe. They paused for an hour or so at the station and citizens were privileged to call on the Royal Entourage. Princess Louise expressed her enthusiasm that Wyoming had granted women the right to vote and to hold office.

As the year grew to a close, Boz told Martha, "I itch to be free of the badge, to settle back and be an ordinary citizen. Yes, I think I'll enjoy being done with risk and gunpowder and lawlessness. A settled man."

But even now, his career of riding for the law was not over. Before the New Year, 1883, dawned, he was called to duty again.

Great herds of cattle graze on the open domain of the Wyoming plains.

Chapter 18

CHIEF DETECTIVE
FOR THE STOCK GROWER'S

Boz knew how all these ranchers felt about the lovely rangelands of southern and eastern Wyoming. They belonged to them. The valleys of the Chugwater, the North Platte, the Laramie, the Sweetwater, the Sybille, and the high mountain plateaus of the Medicine Bows and the Sierra Madres. Up to now the grassland of the Powder River country had been forbidden fruit—Sioux country and although a few white men had dared to intrude, it was at the risk of their scalps. But now the Sioux were gone, and those rangelands beckoned.

By 1883 the cow bonanza was in full swing. Those earlier cowboys, the first on the scene, were reaping the rewards. True, they'd had to be scouts and Indian fighters. But they'd got established—despite the odds.

"Why," C. F. Coffee told N. K., "when I first started cow punching, the buffalo were thinning out and so the red devils ran off whole herds of range cattle and slaughtered them to feed on. Risk? Why, I didn't know I was so tough until I lived through wallowing in snowdrifts at 30 below zero. Of course, it's the cowman's land. We're the fellows that discovered the country."

And there was Hi Kelly, too. He said, "Guess I don't need to tell you how the Indians kept us stirred up all those early years. How we carried guns on our saddles all the time and wouldn't think of going to milk a cow without taking our rifle along."

And Elias Whitcomb, "Just look out there. As far as you can

153

see. It's mine. Just because I haven't got deeds to it, doesn't mean a damn thing. Uncle Sam and I disagree on that. He sent a surveyor out from Washington to peg-stake my land. So I guess him and me are going to run together head on after all."

There were always two sides to every question. Boswell heard the homesteaders' arguments, too. How else was the Territory to be settled—something more than cattle pasture?

And these small settlers were coming in droves to claim their legal limit of land in this veritable paradise. "One hundred sixty acres, no more, no less. That's what we want," they told the big stockmen. "That goes for you same as me—one hundred sixty acres."

A number of the newcomers had already dubbed the early stockmen "Grandees of the Pastoral Acres," and pointed out Ora Haley.

"From butcher boy to cattle baron," they said. "And all in one decade!"

The unmeasured, unfenced grasslands beckoned—pastures and water holes free for the taking. What right did these cow barons—the Eastern men, the Southern men, the Englishmen, the Scots, have to these acres! The newcomers began challenging Horace Plunkett, Richard and Moreton Frewan, Henry Blair, the Swans, John Clay, Francis Warren, the Careys, the Teshcemachers, Fred Hess, Coble and Bosler and Whitaker and many, many more.

As the homesteaders increased, the cattle kings' range decreased. "A bed'll only hold so many occupants," Bob Homer told Boz, "and we were here first."

Other cow barons said the same thing. They wrote the government. "We have priority in this region and the land belongs to us. These newcomers are intruders.

But it was only a short time ago that the Sioux had the same complaint. Chief Crazy Horse and Man-Afraid had protested for the same reason the coming of the first white settlers. "They're driving away our buffalo. They are taking away our hunting grounds. We were here first."

Wrote C. F. Coffee to Boz: "I thought I was the fellow who discovered my ranch, but they sent out a bunch to survey me out of house and home and told me what I could do. So I had to take

154

my medicine. When the granger came, I couldn't shoot him and the only way to get even with him was to go into the banking business, so I did."

But other cattlemen were not so easily persuaded. The settling on the grazing lands infuriated them and tempers on both sides flared red hot. To the big outfits every settler became a rustler. They knew the homesteaders' claims were legal and the only legitimate charge they could hope to make stand up in court was rustling. And there was no doubt about it—the stockmen did have some justification along this line. For cowboys of doubtful reputation were quick to confuse the issue. With great herds turned out on the open range, it was an easy matter for a brand burner to acquire himself a sizeable herd. N. K. had seen too many rustlers operating and knew there was truth in the stockmen's accusations.

"To stop this wanton disrespect of ownership of our members' property," John Clay, big wheel in the Association, proposed, "Let's employ a network of detectives. I've got the right man to head it."

And so Boz received a letter: "With the expanding of the cattle industry in Wyoming, men like me are being robbed blind. The

The government ordered the big cattle outfits to remove their fences for the homesteaders. *Jake Draper collection*

stock growers voted to employ a corp of detectives. We want you for chief."

Heading a network of some eighty sleuths was a real challenge. Boz, in accepting the assignment early in 1883, knew that he'd be away from home much of the time.

"I'll be called into lots of roundups to inspect," he confided to Martha. "I know most of the cattle brands in this country, but now I'll have to be an expert. I'll have to learn all the registered brands in the whole Territory. Some five thousand of them. They're depending on my settling disputed brands, changed brands, and arresting any mavericker!"

So it was a new assignment, but still in his old line—detective work. In June, 1883, Boz was at the Rufe Rhodes roundup. Over 120 men and 900 head of saddle and wagon stock made up this crew.

Old frontiersman Jim Baker, in buckskin garb with Marlin rifle slung on the saddle pommel, came in riding Brownie. It was good to be with Jim again. They'd scouted the Overland Trail a couple of decades earlier. Now Jim was settled on the Snake and owned a fine ranch.

With the gathering, a couple of brown bears were brought in. Jim and Boz roped them and cut them out from the herds. The foreman and cowboys, sitting around the campfire that night, related the amazing prowess of the two frontiersmen.

Famous foreman and old time cowboys gathered for the Rufe Rhode roundup. *Wyoming Stock Growers collection*

"At this roundup were Al Bowie of the Swan-Two-Bar, Ole Missou of the Carey outfit, Sure Shot Latigo, manager for the Trabings, Rooster Wilson, ramrodding for the L7, Chico of the Pick spread, Hookey Carter, using a steel hook strapped to his wrist, as roper for the Hub and Tree. There were other brands, too—the Hog Eye, Sardine Box, Fiddleback, Double Diamond, Duck Bar, Hat, Buzzard, Goose Egg, Camp Stool, Bridle Bit, Lazy H, Bar BC, Flying E, Revolving H, and many more."

Boz, riding in three different roundups that early summer, picked up several brand burners. He had only contempt for these odious artists using their dishonesty to accumulate a herd. Oh, to be sure, they said it about some of the big ranchers, too. He'd heard them tell how "one of the richest of these cattle barons came up the trail with a Texas steer and a branding iron, and three years later was the opulent possessor of several hundred head of fine cattle—the ostensible progeny of that one lone steer."

But back a little while ago, the attitude had been different. So long as the property purloined was Texas longhorns and so long as there was plenty of room on the range, it didn't make too

Inspecting the brands on an organized round-up. Boswell was Chief Detective.
Wyoming Stock Growers collection

much difference. But things had got crowded and the generous attitude toward the nester had changed.

To cope with the rising tide of cattle stealing, Boz was in charge of seeing that the rules of the roundups were carried out, They were held every spring and fall. His was the patient, hazardous job of detection.

"It's a big operation," Boz told his close friend, John McGill, of the Kite. "Riding into the gullies and ravines. Bunching the herds, checking the animals the waddies are roping and branding."

Sometimes Boz would come upon calves with slit tongues. This was a device used by the thieves to deceive the stockmen. The calf did not follow its mother, so its true identity could not be proved. It was the job of Boz and his sleuths to detect these rustlers, flush them out, arrest them and take them into custody for prosecution. His was a vast network with from 25 to 30 roundup districts.

His missions included such orders: "Go to Rawlins and be present to encourage our boys. They must have our full backing in asserting ownership."

Or on a minute's notice, "Be prepared to go East. They've captured a rustler at Lincoln."

From 1883 to 1887, Boz was the Stock Growers' chief. So quietly did he move among these roundups that once he captured three noted outlaws from three different roundups. No one knew the rustlers had been taken into custody.

The powerful Wyoming Stock Growers Association was gaining a reputation. One to be feared by the rustlers. But there was one thing that bothered Boz. Was the Association growing too progressive? Was it moving in directions which would be hard to go along with?

One of the causes for this trend of reasoning was the man who was heading the north country's roundups. He knew Frank Canton well. Canton had been elected sheriff of Johnson County the year Boz retired from Albany County's post. He'd heard rumors of Canton's ambitions.

"Sometimes, ideas run away with people," Boz told the Stock Growers' Secretary, Tom Sturgis. "If only Frank'll keep on an even keel and be sensible. Not get all heated up over the influx of homesteaders that are settling up around Buffalo. Rustlers, yes. Fight them. But the little people who are coming in to settle. Well, I hope he moves with caution."

But Canton, when Boz spoke to him of going slow, retorted. "This Goddamn lawlessness must stop. We'll kill a few of them bastards and have a lot less trouble on our hands."

The trend of affairs was not to the liking of the Chief Detective. The big cow barons resented the settlers encroaching on the open range whether they were rustlers or not. Between the stockmen and the homesteaders there was a growing antagonism.

"Tempers are growing hotter than branding irons." Boz reported to his employer, "And I've no doubt six-guns are hot on both sides."

Boz had little time to spend on his own ranch on the Big Laramie. He had to depend on his foreman to ramrod the spread. It was a rare day that he could ride among his stock. His

N. K.'s ranch on the Big Laramie River where in his later years he entertained many dignitaries. *Minnie Boswell Oviatt collection*

cattle and sheep were bringing a good profit. Some of his young bulls were bringing as much as $800 a piece.

But back in Laramie (yes, the name of the town had been changed in 1884, the City affix had been dropped), Boz would have messages piled up—"Train four new detectives to assist with the Riley Hadsell roundup," or "Please consult with Attorney Riner on old Moore case." Or again it might be: "Report on the P. Boynton and Wray stealing cases," and "Have instructed Ben Morrison to hold cattle until you arrive. We will give bond and take cattle, Tom Sturgis."

Maybe it would be Secretary Sturgis wiring, "Appear before Grand Jury on Dixon case in Fort Collins. It is necessary that this gang of thieves be broken up."

In 1885, Boz was in Sweetwater County with inspectors and deputies for three county roundups—Sweetwater, Carbon and Fremont. Like the trained sleuth he was, he picked up a horse thief and discovered that the outlaw was also wanted for murder in Trinidad, Colorado. Yes, these were busy times.

Yet the small settlers continued to come, fencing their acres and claiming water holes. It was a blazing prelude to trouble.

The cattlemen were taking big losses, not only from rustlers, but from blizzards and drouth and reduced land. They were in a last ditch stand. They were fighting for all they owned and against ruin—cattlemen who'd made the state and endured hardship and dangers were not going to give up without a fight.

There were some mysterious killings up north—dry gulchings—settlers answering their doors at night and being escorted at the point of a gun to some ravine, not to return.

"All this trouble going on worries me," Boz confided to Martha one night, in 1887. He was sitting at his desk fiddling with his badge. "And I've made up my mind. I'm going to turn it in."

And so there in the light of the incandescent rays, he wrote out his resignation as chief of the detectives of the Stock Growers Association. The cattlemen's war would have to blow off without him.

"I'll stay on the Executive Committee," he wrote Secretary T. B. Adams, "and try in any way to help you out."

His resignation was accepted "with great regret," October 28, 1887. And so Boz began planning for a quieter life. He

The ranch of Cattle Kate and Jim Averill on the Sweetwater.

busied himself taking over the ranch operations—his rich pastures dotted with blooded Herefords and Shorthorns. A cavvy of fine horses. And sheep, too. He'd brought his flock in as early as 1879. Oh, to be sure, he knew how most of his cattlemen friends felt about sheep. He'd seen the look in the eyes of a cowman when he asked a man if he also ran sheep. He could sense the growing antagonism brewing between sheepmen and cattlemen.

The next two years Boz remained on the Board of the Stock Growers Association. But he was not always in accord with some of its decisions. He fretted about the brewing feud and he worried about his old comrade of the badge, Frank Canton, up in the north country showing hot headedness. Appeared to be mixed up with a number of questionable escapades. And Mike Shonsey, foreman of the Line Riders, proclaiming impartiality, but his allegiance was still with the Guthrie and Oskamp Cattle Company.

The situation was becoming serious. The big cattle outfits were fuming over ranges being cut up into small holdings and the continual influx of the settlers. John Clay, president of the Association, told Boz, "We're going to arm for one last ditch stand."

161

"This feuding," Boz told Clay, "will have to get along without me."

He'd barely gone off the Executive Board when a new kind of violence flared. Over in the Sweetwater country were the open ranges claimed by the Bothwell brothers, John Clay, Fred Hesse and Tom Sun and their associates. Here a man named Jim Averill settled, opening a small store and saloon. A woman, Ella Watson (or Kate Maxwell, as she signed herself), more commonly known as Cattle Kate, took up an adjoining homestead. Gradually, the woman's lands were becoming stocked with cattle—some claiming she traded her favors to the cowboys for cows of various brands. At any rate, the homestead ate into the very heart of the cattlemen's kingdom.

It was a day in July, 1889, when all the country was shocked

Cattle Kate was dragged from her cabin on the Sweetwater and hanged by irate stockmen. *Wyoming Stock Growers collection*

by the lynchings—Ella Watson and Jim Averill—in a coulee of Spring Creek.

"Ten of the Stockmen did it," the newspaper said. The coroner's inquest stated that "the two came to their deaths at the hands of A. J. Bothwell, Tom Sun, John Durbin, R. M. Galbraith, Bud Connor, E. McLain and one unknown man."

"I just can't believe they'd hang a woman in Wyoming." Boz said. Many worried about the effect the lynching of a female would have on Wyoming Territory's petition for statehood in Washington.

Jim Averill who was lynched with Cattle Kate on the Sweetwater.

Archives-Western History Center, University of Wyoming

So now, in 1890, there was an air of anxiety. Eastern papers were protesting the supremacy of mob law in the wild wilderness of Wyoming. Surely the United States government could not overlook this recent insurrection and grant statehood!

It took all the persuasion of the Territory's two popular senators, Francis E. Warren and Joseph Carey, to win their colleagues' votes. But on July 10, 1890, Wyoming came in as the forty-fourth state. And it came in with woman suffrage to become known as "The Equality State."

But becoming a state did not put a stop to the war for the grasslands.

Chapter 19

BOZ DIFFERS WITH THE RANGE KINGS

As far as the big outfits, and especially those backed with foreign capital were concerned, the fight had just begun. Boz couldn't help noticing that the stockmen were more interested in securing good gunmen now.

Sheriff Red Angus up in the north country told him, "They don't give a damn about a man's qualifications as a cowboy. Just as long as he can shoot."

And so ghosts armed with Winchesters and Carbines rode the ranges. And Phantoms crept along the Wyoming trails. The rhythm of horses' hooves reminded Boz of the cadences of drumbeats of old warriors, rising and falling. There were troubled times ahead. In Laramie he read about these violent happenings all over the state and fervently hoped that peace might still come.

There was the lynching of Tom Waggoner in June, 1891, over near Newcastle. Four men called at his door and asked him to accompany them. There were other dry gulchings. Homesteaders who'd come into the country and threatened the ranges. In November, Orley Jones and Johnny Tisdale, two well-liked punchers, were killed—in almost the same manner.

Boz and his old friend Phil Mandel, meeting on the street one day, discussed the rumors of how Tisdale had been shot in the back, and his blood was all over the Christmas gifts he'd bought for his kids.

"They've got a real bull, roaring and seeing red, up there in the north country." Phil said, "Crazy Goddamn sonsabitches!"

"They've really set off a keg of dynamite," Boz agreed.

And now the stockmen were planning an expedition and a military march into the Powder River country. They invited Boz to join them. "You're going too far with this and nothing good will come of it," he told them, declining their invitation.

April 6, 1892, two days after the Stock Growers meeting, a mysterious train pulled in from Denver to Cheyenne, then headed northward. Aboard were Texas gunmen, and Boz was surprised to learn that some of his old frontier comrades, now prosperous ranchers, were going with them.

Reverberations of this daring attack were heard all over Wyoming. The old order was fighting for its very life, hell-bent on driving the encroachers out.

The invasion of Johnson County, as this was called, came to a disastrous end, and resulted in much embarrassment to the cow kings. When the body of Nate Champion, with eight bullet holes through him, and Nick Ray's remains, charred and burned beyond recognition, were brought into Buffalo, the citizens were in an uproar. True, these two had been labeled rustlers and were at the top of the "Dead List" of the Invaders. But the method of riddance was a black blot on Wyoming.

Governor Barber telegraphed President Harrison that Wyoming was in a state of insurrection. Troops were ordered in. The stockmen and their hired Texas gunmen were locked up

Cattlemen "Invaders" in the Johnson County War were confined to the penitentiary across the Laramie River. Here Boz had an opportunity to interview them.   *Wyoming Stock Growers collection*

at Fort McKinney near Buffalo. Certainly a number of the cattlemen now realized they'd made a big mistake. They had a chance to cool off their tempers and think it over as they were transported back to Cheyenne and locked up at Fort Russell. Back on home ground they were in less danger of counterattack from the Defenders. Here, too, the Stock Growers Association was known for its powerfulness.

On July 2, 1892, forty-four of the Invaders were brought into Laramie and Judge Blake ordered them committed to the north wing of the penitentiary across the river. Here, during their two weeks' confinement, Boz had a chance to talk with them and hear their story. Damned fools!

There were many delays and postponements in bringing the stockmen to trial. Finally, Sheriff Red Angus confided, "Johnson County is plumb broke. It can't possibly pay the $100 a day to keep the Invaders locked up 'til trial time."

So one by one, the cow barons were out, free on bond or paroled. Some of them left the country. At least a couple of them had nervous breakdowns.

Martha Salisbury Boswell and her sisters, Jenny Pope and Annette Butler.
Henry Pope collection

The Boswell home, Fifth and Grand, was moved from Fort Sanders when the outpost was abandoned. Moved again it now serves as a Community Center at LaBonte park.

Tom Horn, hired by the big cattle outfits was hanged in Cheyenne, in 1903 for the killing of the young boy, Willie Nickell.

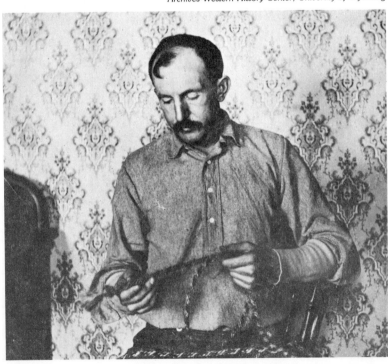

And it certainly hadn't stopped the nesters. They kept right on coming. And so the violence of the ranges still clung to the land.

But now Boz had other things on his mind. Martha. He'd come home one evening to the cottage on Fifth Street and found her in bed where Dr. Finfrock had ordered her to remain.

"Her heart," the medico told him, shaking his head. "It's been coming on for some time. Maybe as long as fifteen years."

And then it was 1893. And Martha was dead. Silent, stunned with grief, Boz wired her mother and brother in Elkhorn. They'd be in on Number Three for the services.

The funeral was a big one. People overflowed the white cottage on Fifth and Grand, and out into the yard. Neighbors and friends came to comfort Boz and Minnie. "You must live for the living," they consoled husband and daughter.

Yes, he must remember his promise to Martha. He must pick up the tag ends of his life and carry on.

Losing Martha changed Boz. Time moved slower and nothing seemed important now. Even the cattlemen's troubles. Oh yes, to be sure, it had flared up again. There were scars left by the Johnson County War, but the cattlemen had risen again, intent on exterminating this new intruding civilization. When they struck this time, it was with a hired assassin—Tom Horn.

Uneasiness grew with the knowledge that a calloused killer stalked the land. There was Matt Rush, eating his lonely meal in a line cabin, shot dead. And Bill Lewis, dry-gulched at his Iron Mountain ranch in the heart of John Coble's cow kingdom, killed in his corral. And the whiz of an assassin's bullet bore down on Fred Powell in his hay meadow on Horse Creek one September morning.

"Sure, Horn's horse was fagged when he rode into the livery stable," Officer Charles Yund, now Albany County Sheriff, told Boz, "but who could say Tom Horn did the killing?"

The murder of Powell hit Boz hard. His concern was for the widow, pretty Mary Keene, for he'd watched her grow from a babe to young womanhood in Laramie City. She'd married Fred Powell and moved to the Horse Creek homestead. Mary refused to leave her acreages after her husband's murder. She and her young son, Willie, swore they would fight to the death, if necessary, their right to remain. And they did.

There was no doubt about it—Horn was creating a figure of terror. He had his theory on how to halt the over-crowding of the open range. "I'm an exterminatin' sonofabitch."

Then one day in July, 1901, there was one killing too many. Kels Nickell, ignoring the cattlemen's warning, had brought a flock of sheep to his homestead on Iron Mountain. The cowmen were furious. On that summer day, thirteen-year-old Willie Nickell rode out of his father's corral to see how "the woolies" were making it at camp. He was shot and killed.

The murderer apparently mistook the boy for the father, Kels. And the Terror of the Range had proof once more he was not in the Nickell vicinity. His alibi—he was enroute to Denver with a load of bucking horses for a rodeo. But that night in a bar on Blake Street, he made the mistake of his life. He got drunk and bragged: "That Goddamned Nickell shot was the best I ever made and the dirtiest trick I ever done!"

United States Marshal Joe Le Fors was advised of his bragging. He trapped Horn into a full confession while they were visiting a back room of a Cheyenne saloon.

There was a murder trial in Wyoming's capital, and Tom Horn, one of the last of the badmen, was sentenced to hang. It was a cold blustery day in November, 1903, when Horn was "put in a wooden overcoat" and the lid was closed on his career. The sigh of relief could be heard all over Wyoming.

But before Boz was to see the frontier settle down, he was to observe another range war. "Sheep," the catttlemen cried. "Sheep in too large bands are ruining our grazing lands."

For a couple of decades, this new hatred blazed between cowmen and sheep growers. Removed from the scene now, he was a spectator watching the trouble brew. He read of the raid in the Tensleep country in 1909 when Joe Allemand and his herders were shot, killed and burned to death as they camped with their flocks on the No Water Creek.

In his home county, except for some feuding in the Tie Siding area, there had been little trouble between the cattlemen and sheep growers. In fact, in the early days of his ranching, Boz had been one of the first to bring sheep in to graze with his cattle on the meadows of the Boswell ranch. No one had challenged his right then.

Since the early days, cattle and horse herds and flocks of sheep, as well, grazed on the rich meadows of his Big Laramie spread. It was a man's right to decide what he'd raise. Would the frontier never learn this lesson? Would it never learn patience and neighborliness? He recalled again what Jim McNasser told him a long time ago—the day he decided to make this highland his home. "The altitude does something to men's tempers. Triggers them quick to fire and burn."

Probably when Wyoming had a few more years' experience on its shoulders, it would settle down to a benign and peaceful existence.

"The sooner these fellows realize there's room here in Wyoming for all of us, the sooner we settle down," he told Minnie one night. "Now I guess that types me. I guess you'd say it means only one thing, Minnie. Your father is getting old."

Boz on his fine mount at the ranch corral on The Big Laramie River.

The famous picture-maker W. H. Jackson visited the site of Fort Sander in the '20's. All that remained were the decaying stone guardhouse and another building.

Chapter 20

A LAWMAN FOREVER

Yes, Boz was getting old and his activities were slowed down. For him it was almost like being a spectator at Chauncey Root's Opera House—watching a new scene unfold. Gone were they all now—those old mountain men in buckskins, cavalrymen in dusty blue, scouts hawk-eyed and trail shrewd, buffalo hunters, stage coach drivers, bullwhackers and mule skinners.

Yes, it seemed a very long time ago he and his companions had ridden forth on a chill grey morning to join that caravan heading west—"Pike's Peak or Bust!"

And all those Indian fights with the Apaches, the Pawnees, the Utes, the Arapahoes and Cheyennes. And his last ride against the Sioux with General George Crook.

Practically all the early landmarks of Laramie, too, were gone. A University town, now, its rolling campus displacing the town's second cemetery. And its downtown changed—even the streets renamed. Boz was glad the citizens had paid homage to that gallant old soldier who'd ridden out to meet death at the hands of the Utes back in '79. "A" Street, they'd rechristened Thornburgh.

Oh, a lot of changes had taken place, mostly for the good. Boz knew the town like a book, and every spot held a memory for him, some happy, some tragic. Sometimes when the new generation asked him to point early day sites to them, the shadows of the past danced in front of his eyes, and he had to shake his head

Buffalo Bill Cody vacationed between Wild West shows at the Boswell ranch. He and Boz were close friends.

to get the cobwebs out of it. Yes, Laramie City had been a rip-snorter in its day!

And out to the south, beneath the suns of summer and the snows of winter, lay the ruins of that outpost of this civilization, Fort Sanders. The stone skeletons of its guardhouse with iron bars reminding him of the lawless wild men he'd locked inside. A few frame buildings still leaned like broken hulks of sinking ships against the rolling skies. The grasses had long grown over the emptied graves. Meadow larks and gopher holes, and wild blue lupine to match the late afternoon skies, carpeted the old parade ground where once woman sat beneath parasols, listening to Nevotti's Fourth Infantry band.

And the range grass was gone, too. That is, the tall grass. The grass that had made of this land a veritable battlefield. The grass that the white man had wrested from the Sioux. The grass that the homesteaders had won from the range kings. The grass

"Teddy" Roosevelt arrives in Laramie, Memorial Day, 1903. Boz, as marshal of the day, is on horse beside carriage.

Western History Center, University of Wyoming

that the sheepmen had taken from the cowmen. The grass that had been knee-high to a cavalry horse when Boz came here.

Gone, too, were most of his old comrades. For twenty years now out on his Laramie River ranch, he'd played host to notables—Teddy Roosevelt, Buffalo Bill, English and Scottish lords, senators and congressmen and governors. And if a President of the United States favored Wyoming with a visit, Boz was chosen to be escort and marshal for the party.

That Memorial Day in 1903, he'd been designated official host for the newly inaugurated President, Teddy Roosevelt. The highlight of that event was the ride from Laramie to Cheyenne. The mounts carefully selected by Boz were changed three times in the fifty-mile trek. First relay was at old Tie City at the head of Happy Jack Canyon. Teddy was spellbound with the scenery, and the tales Boz told of early day skirmishes between timber choppers and the red devils.

Again, on a beautiful autumn day in 1911, Boz was assigned

Marshal for President Roosevelt's horseback trek from Laramie to Cheyenne, Memorial Day, 1903. Boswell is fourth from left.

Western History Center, University of Wyoming

to the committee to receive President William Howard Taft who'd come to visit Laramie. It was here at the new city park, Undine, that the President spoke to the school children.

The city fathers invited Boz to be in the Mayor's party when Woodrow Wilson scheduled a platform speech that November day in 1919. That's how Boz knew first-hand why the President hadn't made his promised oration on the League of Nations. The President was gravely ill when Boz called on him in the private railroad car. Two days later, Wilson was stricken with paralysis which invalided him for the remainder of his term.

Yes, Boz thanked the citizens—they were generous tendering him all these honors. Yet it was on his ranch on the Big Laramie he loved most to be. Here, with Minnie, a charming hostess, he entertained old and new friends. His grandkids and grand nieces and nephews found him a real delight. The fine old

Minnie Boswell Oviatt, only child of Martha and N. K. Boswell.

Archives-Western History Center. University of Wyoming

ranch was an exciting place—streams full of trout, hills full of deer and his barns full of saddle horses.

One thing Boz wouldn't tolerate, was any monkey business when it came to his animals. His wrangler, Joe Fredericks, found this out the day he tin-canned a hapless mule that'd trespassed into the horse corral. The tormented creature came whirling over the rails, hurdled the new Franklin Boz was trying out, and landed in a huddle in the road.

Boz, faster than lightning, was confronting his hired hand. "You're fired. Here's your pay. Get your saddle and bedroll and get going."

Charlie Oviatt, Minnie's husband, was doing a good job running the big spread. Verdant meadows richly irrigated feeding blooded stock.

Here, in the winter when the leaves fell from the giant cottonwoods, Boz had a view to the river where on weekends the kids skated or sledded down the slopes. Sometimes he took the young ones arrowhead hunting and sometimes, shading his eyes, he looked out over this country inflamed by a late sunset and he

Clarence and Martha Oviatt, grandchildren of the famed peace officer.

Courtesy Harold Hunt

talked about the trails he'd blazed, and he showed them the Indian sign meaning coyote—stroking his brow and raising two forked fingers.

There were occasions during these last years when the citizens called on him to review some exploit from those stirring early days. Like the commemoration in 1916, when University of Wyoming's renowned historian, Dr. Grace Raymond Hebard, arranged a program to dedicate old Camp Walbach. The date had been set for 1914, but storms delayed it two years. Now in 1916, the program was re-scheduled with the Honorable Ex-Governor of Wyoming, Joseph M. Carey, making the principal speech. Then he introduced Boswell, whose "Reminiscences" were recorded by the Oregon Trail Commission.

"It was a long time ago," Boz told his audience that day in September. "Back when Hi Kelly and I were employed by the United States government as scouts for a time during the winter

World War I Memorial, downtown Laramie, site of Boz's last historic ceremonial appearance. *Western History Center, University of Wyoming*

used for protection by the immigrants traveling over Cheyenne Pass on the Lodge Pole Trail—Fort Laramie to Denver.) Boz then spoke of the skirmish "that year when the Indians came upon us, their arrows thick and fast filling the air. We were barricaded inside the sandstone walls, and I remember saying to Hi, 'Hope our luck holds.' Just as we were thanking our stars we'd come through without a scratch, an arrow ripped my shoulder. Still got that scar. We buried sixteen soldiers that year—reports said they died from eating tainted soup. A few immigrants' final resting place was there, too, marked by crude red stones, but only three remain."

When Boz finished his talk, Governor Carey unveiled the stone memorial. A piece of granite to mark a lonely outpost in the long ago wilderness—Camp Walbach.

Then 1921 rolled around. Laramie was having a celebration—the Laramie Plains Roundup, a three day festival. It was scheduled to commence on the fourth, but a rain postponed it to the fifth. The day dawned, a day when the celebrants lapsed into languid easiness under the warm Wyoming sun.

In the intersection of Thornburgh and Second, a podium nudged the impressive World War One bronze statue dedicated to the boys in khaki. A band was playing, the lately discharged veterans marched and the cowboys on prancing mounts brought up the rear of the parade. Sheriff George Trabing, son of Boz's now departed comrade Gus, was escorting Mary Godat Bellamy to a place on the platform. They were honoring her today—for her service in the state legislature.

Along the street women in big hats stood in clusters exchanging pleasantries. Kids in their Sunday best, wide-eyed and lip licking, gazed longingly at the ice cream soda fountain inside. A. T. Williams' Candy Parlor. Men rubbed shoulder to shoulder and gabbed about the price of two-year-olds and the new machinery down at the roundhouse. Cronies, that is those that were left of the old frontier, swapped yarns.

"When I stopped off at Tie Siding back in '68," Ed Ivinson said, "It was with a load of molasses bound for the West Coast. Then a barrel of sorghum hit that good-for-nothing fellow."

"Broke his leg as I remember," Billie Owen put in. "Sued you, didn't he?"

"Sure did. But a hell of a lot of good it did him."

"Yah," John McGlll spoke up, "More'n one's found that out. Like I always said, Ed Ivinson can sell a whore house to an Episcopalian bishop!"

They all laughed. Then Bill Holliday put in. "Remember those log drives! There were no better logs, damned few as good, as them we floated down from Woods Landing. Gives you a good feeling just remembering how shy of knots they were. And fresh pitch smell. Nothing like it these days."

Tom Alsop, pastures full of fatted calves, joined in too about roundup days when the waddies were riding and roping. And yelling prayer words, but not meaning the same.

Boz was standing quietly. A lean, sinewy old man, white mustachioed and bearded, weather leathered face, his piercing eyes with the glint of steel. Straight as an arrow and as rangy as a wild mustang that has fed long on prairie grass, in his eighties now he still handled himself with the agility of a Sioux chieftain. Etched on his face, too, was a pattern of wrinkles that told of life's experiences—love, hate, exploits, daring. A desire to survive in a hard land.

The red, white and blue bunting was waving faintly in the breeze. The speaker was scanning the crowd. And then he spotted Boz. "We have with us today, N. K. Boswell. Boz is knit to us with a tie of comradeship and respect which endures with increasing love each year. His influence stretches across this land, for he was a vanguard of a people on the move into this frontier of desolation and savagery."

Boz shifted uneasily. It always embarrassed him when people singled him out with praise. He was thinking—all these people living in peace at last.

The Indian wars were over. The cattlemen's feuds done. Now here it was —his town—at last, the way Martha and he had envisioned it—a fine modern college city and the hub of the railroad and livestock industries, too—its people all pulling together. And out there on the Laramie Plains, ranchers—sheep and cattle—big and little, lived in peace, good neighbors. Somehow today, he felt it in his bones—that this was his last summer. He turned to face the speaker again. "Boz," the commentator was saying, "was one of the greatest lawmen of the old

West. And there's his daughter, Minnie, and her husband, our county's Senator Oviatt. And maybe some of you remember Mrs. Boswell, singing her songs and mothering us. She was the ministering angel at St. Joseph the time the rolling mills blew up."

The steady penetrating eyes of old Boz took on a faint trace of mist. There was no glint of steel in them now. Only the gleam of reminiscing as he gazed again past the orator, past the crowd, out toward the blue horizon. And on his face were the marks of the land.

Yes, he must have had a premonition that day that his work was done. That he was handing this land over to them—to all these people—the inheritors.

On October 12, 1921, the Laramie *Republican Boomerang* wrote: "N. K. Boswell, bravest of the pioneers is dead."

The long funeral cortege moved from the downtown church, along Grand Avenue with its fine homes, past the University campus and to Greenhill Cemetery. Hundreds lined the street, bared heads, somber reflective eyes. Here, passing before them, was the last link of that old wild West. But Laramie's lawman would always live in their memory as a symbol of the breed of men who tamed the frontier.

THE END.

BIBLIOGRAPHY

Books:

Bancroft, Hubert H., *History of Nevada, Colorado and Wyoming*, The History Publishing Company, San Francisco, 1898

Bartlett, I. S., *History of Wyoming, Vol. Two*, S. J. Clarke Publishing Co., Chicago, 1918

Brayer, Herbert, *The Influence of British Capital on the Western Range Cattle Industry. Westerners Brand Book, No. IV, No. V*, Denver

Brown, Jesse, and Willard, A.M., *The Black Hills Trails*, Rapid City Journal Company, Rapid City, South Dakota, 1924

Brown, Mark H., and Felton, W. R., *The Frontier Years*, Henry Holt & Co., New York, 1955

Burns, Robert Homer, Gillespie, Andrew Springs, and Richardson, Willing Gay, *Wyoming's Pioneer Ranches*, Top of the World Press, 1955

Burt, Struthers, *Powder River Let'er Buck*, Farrar & Rinehart, New York, 1938

Canton, Frank, *Frontier Tales, the Autobiography of Frank M. Canton*, Houghton-Mifflin Co., Boston, 1930

Cook, D. J. and John W., *D. J. Cook Superintendent of Rocky Mountain Detective Association*, 1882

Cook, D. J., *Hands Up*, Oklahoma University Press, Norman, 1958

Collier, William Ross and Westrate, Edwin Victor, *Dave Cook of the Rockies*, Rufus Rockwell Wilson, New York, 1936

Cowan, Bud, *Range Rider*, Doubleday & Doran, New York, 1930

Greenburg, Dan W., *Sixty Years, a Brief Review of Wyoming Cattle Days*, Cheyenne, 1933

Elston, Allan Vaughan, *Gun Law in Laramie*, J. B. Lippincott, Co., Philadelphia and New York, 1959

King, Col. Charles, *General Crook*, Armitage and Allen, 1891

Linford, Velma, *Wyoming Frontier State*, Old West Publishing Co., Denver, 1947

Love, Robertus, *The Rise and Fall of Jessie James*, G. P. Putnam's Sons, New York, 1926

Mercer, A. S., *The Banditti of the Plains*, privately published, Cheyenne, 1894

Mokler, Alfred James, *History of Natrona County, Wyoming, 1888-1922*, Chicago, 1923

Monaghan, Jay, *The Last of the Badmen*, the Bobbs Merril Co., New York, 1946

Pence, Mary Lou and Homsher, Lola M., *The Ghost Towns of Wyoming*, Hastings House Publishers, New York, 1956

Raine, William MacLeod, *Famous Sheriffs and Western Outlaws*, Garden City Publishing Company, New York, 1929

Rankin, M. Wilson, *Reminiscences of Frontier Days*

Rollinson, John K., *Wyoming Cattle Trails*, Caxton Printers, Caldwell, Idaho, 1948

Sabin, Edwin L., *Wild Men of the West*, Thomas Y. Crowell, New York, 1929
Building the Union Pacific, Lippincott, New York, 1919

Sandoz, Mari, *The Cattlemen*, Hastings House Publishers, New York, 1958

Shores, A. W. (Doc), *The Autobiography of a Lawman*

Spring, Agnes Wright, *Seventy Years of the Cow Country*, Cheyenne, 1942
Cheyenne and Black Hills Stage and Express Routes, Arthur H. Clark, Glendale, California

Thompson, John Charles, *The Hanging of Tom Horn*, Brand Book, Westerners, Denver, 1945

Triggs, J. H., *History and Directory of Laramie City, Wyoming Territory*, Daily Sentinel, Laramie, 1875
History of Cheyenne and Northern Wyoming, Herald Book Publishing Co., Omaha, Nebraska, 1876

Vaughn, J. W., *With Crook at the Rosebud*, The Stackpole Co., Harrisburg, Pennsylvania, 1956

Wellman, Paul I., *The Indian Wars of the West*, Doubleday & Co., New York, 1947

Whitcomb, E. W., *Reminiscences of a Pioneer*, Biennial Report of State History, Wyoming, 1920

Whittenburg, Clarice, *Wyoming's People*, Old West Publishing Co., Denver, 1958

Wisconsin, American Guide Series, Duell, Sloan and Pearce, New York, 1941

Wyoming, A Guide to Its History, Highways and People, Oxford University Press, New York, 1941

Young, Col. Harry, *Hard Knocks*, Laird and Lee Inc. Publishers, Chicago, 1915

Newspapers, Periodicals and Records:

Albany County Records, Proceedings of County Commissioners, 1870 to 1883, Albany County Courthouse, Laramie, Wyoming

Bancroft, H. H., film, Personal Letters from Wyoming Pioneers, N. K. Boswell, Bancroft Library, Berkley, California, 1885

Carbon County Journal, 1880-1881, Carbon County Museum, Rawlins, Wyoming

Carbon County Records, Court Transcript Case of Territory of Wyoming versus George Parrotte, Clerk of Court Office, Carbon County, Rawlins, Wyoming

Casper Daily Mail, 1889

Census Reports, Walworth County, Elkhorn, Wisconsin, State Historical Society of Wisconsin, Madison

Census Reports, Laramie City, 1870

Elkhorn Independent, April 3, 1867

Frazer, Marie Milligan, Some Phases of the History of the Union Pacific Railroad in Wyoming, unpublished thesis, University of Wyoming, Coe Library

Frontier Days—The Vigilance Committee, W. L. Kuykendall, J. M. and L. W. Kuykendall Publishers, 1917

Frontier Index 1868 Microfilm fragmentary, Bancroft Library, Berkley, California

Greenhill Cemetery Burial Records, City of Laramie, Wyoming

Hebard, Grace Raymond, The First Woman Jury, The Journal of American History, Fourth Quarterly, Indiana and New York, 1913

Jackson, W. Turrentine, The Wyoming Stock Growers Association Political Power in Wyoming Territory, Mississippi Valley Historical Review XXX, March, 1947

Laramie Boomerang 1882 to 1932. Coe Library, University of Wyoming, Laramie, Wyoming

Laramie Sentinel, 1875 to 1881, Coe Library University of Wyoming, Laramie, Wyoming

Newcastle Journal, June 19, 1891 (Wyoming)

Owens, W. O. Personal file, Archives and Western History Department, University of Wyoming, Laramie, Wyoming

Pacific Reporter, Vol. 73, Horn versus Supreme Court of Wyoming, St. Paul West Publishing Co. 1903

Rawlins Daily Times, Wyoming, May 12, 1960

State Leader, Cheyenne, February 1925

State of Wyoming versus Tom Horn, Clerk of Court office, Laramie County, Cheyenne, Wyoming

Union Pacific Magazine, November 1926

Union Pacific Magazine, Tales from Old Times, A. P. Wood

Walworth County, Elkhorn, Wisconsin. Registrar of Deeds Marriage Record 1859, Martha Salisbury and Nathaniel Boswell

Wyoming State Historical Department, Annals of Wyoming, Cheyenne, Wyoming

Wyoming Stock Growers Association Records on file in Archives and Western History Library, University of Wyoming, Laramie, Wyoming